Living Free

Abridged Edition

(A Sequel to *Born Free*)

by JOY ADAMSON

SCHOLASTIC BOOK SERVICES
NEW YORK • TORONTO • LONDON • AUCKLAND • SYDNEY • TOKYO

All the photographs in this book were taken at Elsa's camp in Kenya by the Adamsons.

Copyright © 1961 by Joy Adamson. This abridged edition is published by Scholastic Book Services, a division of Scholastic Magazines, Inc., by arrangement with Harcourt Brace Jovanovich, Inc.

10th printing .... November 1974

Printed in the U.S.A.

CONTENTS

To all wild animals and their freedom

All the experiences recounted in this book were shared with my husband, George, and it could not have been written without him. I would like to acknowledge my gratitude to everyone who, whether in an official or a private capacity, made it possible for us to spend so much time at Elsa's camp.—J.A.

Introduction

JOY ADAMSON, the author, is married to the Senior Game Warden of the Northern Frontier Province of Kenya. George Adamson's duties consist primarily in controlling and protecting wild life in this area. If animals cause injury to Africans and their livestock, it is his responsibility to remove the menace; if there are reports of poaching in the reserves where wild animals have their sanctuary, it is his duty to bring the poachers to justice and to enforce the Game Laws.

The Adamsons live at Isiolo, a small township one hundred and eighty miles from Nairobi, but George's work entails constant patrolling of the vast area under his supervision. In *Born Free*, her first book about Elsa the lioness, Joy Adamson describes how her husband went out to shoot a man-eating lion, was charged by a lioness, killed her in self-defense, and then, realizing that she must recently have given birth, searched for her cubs and ended by bringing home three little lionesses only a few days old.

The "Big One," Lustica, and Elsa were cared for by Joy until her husband found that three fully grown lionesses would make daily life and constant safaris very difficult. The "Big One" and Lustica thereupon went to the Rotterdam-Blydorp Zoo.

Elsa, the smallest of the three, remained with the Adamsons and shared their daily life; she went on patrol with them, joined in their hunting, fishing, and bathing expeditions, and became an affectionate and dignified member of the Adamson household. She was devoted to Joy and George, and very fond of three members of their African staff: Nuru, Makedde, and Ibrahim.

When Elsa was nearly fully grown, the Adamsons began to feel that she was being denied part of her natural heritage. They determined to attempt what had never before been tried: to re-educate Elsa for life in the bush. This meant teaching a domesticated lioness to kill, to associate with wild lions, and generally to lead a free, independent life among the dangers of natural conditions.

The first attempt at release proved unsuccessful. The climate of the area chosen by the Adamsons did not agree with Elsa, and she became ill. Besides, she showed herself shy of the wild lions of the region, unable to provide for herself, and unwilling to be parted from her foster parents.

Undefeated, the Adamsons took Elsa to another area, in Meru Game Reserve, one hundred and fifty miles distant from Isiolo. There, in country ideally suited for a lion's home, near a large river lined with trees and a huge ridge of rock with cliffs and caves, Elsa was released a second time. Commuting between Isiolo and their camp on the Ura River, Joy and George, with infinite patience, taught Elsa to become independent. As time passed, she learned to hunt, to defend her kill against predators, and to associate freely with the lions of the area. Yet in spite of this return to natural life in the wild, and against all predictions and expectations, Elsa remained on close, affectionate terms with her human family. She visited the Adamsons each time they came to camp near her. The incredible was achieved: Elsa had become a lioness at home in two worlds. *Born Free* ended with the Adamsons returning from their camp to Isiolo, knowing that their experiment had been successful and that Elsa had found a wild mate.

Living Free is the story of Elsa and her cubs.

—THE PUBLISHERS

AUTHOR'S NOTE: Since Elsa's cubs were born I have kept notes in which I have recorded what we observed of Elsa and her family when we were in camp. *Living Free* is based on these notes.—J.A.

Mother and cub.

Elsa Mates with a Wild Lion

IT was between August 29 and September 4, 1959, that my husband, George, actually saw Elsa and her lion courting.

On his return to Isiolo he told me what he had seen. I could hardly bear not to start off for camp alone, for I was afraid that Elsa might now follow her mate into a world beyond our reach.

But when we arrived she was there waiting for us, by the Big Rock close to the car track.

She was very affectionate, and also very hungry.

As our tents were being pitched, her lion started calling; and during the night he circled around the camp while she remained with George, eating heartily and quite uninterested in her mate's appeal. At dawn we heard the lion still calling, but from much farther away.

For two days she remained in camp, eating so enormously that she was too sleepy to move till the afternoon, when she went out fishing with George.

During the third night she ate so much that we were quite worried about her; yet in the morning, in spite of her bulging belly, she trotted into the bush with us and stalked two jackals and then a flock of guinea fowl. Of course, each time she closed in on them they flew off, whereupon she sat down and licked her paws.

On our walk home Elsa, full of high spirits and affection, rolled me over several times in the sand, while I listened to the trumpeting of elephants which were much too close for my liking.

That night she slept in front of my tent, but just before dawn her lion started calling and she went off in his direction.

Their calls were easy to distinguish. Elsa had a very deep guttural voice, but after her initial roar only gave two or three whuffing grunts, whereas her lion's voice was less deep, and after his roar he always gave at least ten or twelve grunts.

During Elsa's absence we broke camp and left for Isiolo, hoping that she was in the company of her mate. We were able to return to the camp on October 10.

It was three weeks since we had left Elsa. An hour after our arrival we saw her swimming across the river to greet us, but instead of the exuberant welcome she usually gave us, she walked slowly up to me. She did not seem to be hungry, and was exceptionally gentle and quiet.

Patting her, I noticed that her skin had become extremely soft and her coat unusually glossy. She was pregnant. There was no doubt about it. She must have conceived about a month ago. This meant that the cubs might arrive between December 15 and 21.

It is widely believed that a pregnant lioness, who is handicapped in hunting by her condition, is helped by one or two other lionesses who act as "aunts." They are also supposed to assist in looking after the newborn cubs, for the male is not of much practical use on such occasions and, indeed, is often not allowed near the young lions for some weeks.

Since poor Elsa had no "aunts," it would be our job to replace them. George and I talked over plans to help to feed her and avoid any risk of her injuring herself during her pregnancy.

I was to stay in camp as much as I could, and at the nearest Game Scout post, some twenty-five miles away, we would establish a herd of goats from which I could collect a few in my truck at regular intervals.

Nuru would remain with me to help with Elsa, Makedde would guard us with his rifle, Ibrahim could drive, and I would keep one boy, the Toto (the word *toto* means "child" in Swahili[1]), to act as personal servant.

George would visit us as often as his work allowed.

As though she had understood our conversation, Elsa hopped onto my camp bed as soon as it was made ready, and looked as if she thought it the only suitable place for someone in her condition.

Next morning, as I did not feel well, I had the bed carried down to the studio (a place on the riverbank overhung by the branches of a large tree where I work), and

[1] One of the languages spoken in central and southern Africa.

Elsa came to share it with me. This was uncomfortable, so after a time I tipped it over and rolled her off. This indignity caused her to retire, offended, into the river reeds till the late afternoon, when it was time for our walk.

I observed that her movements were very slow, and that even the noise of elephants close by only made her cock her ears. That night she rested in George's tent, unresponsive to the call of a lion who seemed to be very near the camp. As in the early morning the lion was still calling, we took Elsa for a walk in his direction. There, to our surprise, we found the spoor of *two* lions.

When she began to show an interest in these pugmarks we left her and returned home. She did not come back that night, so we were surprised to hear a lion grunting extremely close to the camp. (Indeed, in the morning his pugmarks proved that he had been within ten yards of our tent.) The next day Elsa again stayed away. Hoping to make the lions kindly disposed toward her, George shot a buck and left it as a farewell gift; then we returned to Isiolo.

After we had spent two weeks at home we decided that it was time to go back and see Elsa.

It was dark when we reached camp, but she appeared within a few moments. She was extremely thin, very hungry, and had deep, bleeding gashes and bites on her neck, and also the claw marks of a lion on her back. While she gnawed at the meat we had brought and I dressed her wounds, she responded by licking me and rubbing her head against mine.

During the night we heard her dragging the carcass

down to the river and splashing across with it, and later we heard her returning. Shortly afterward some baboons gave an alarm and were answered by a lion across the river. Elsa replied from our side with soft moans. Very early in the morning she tried to force her way through the wicker door of the thorn enclosure which surrounded my tent. She pushed her head half through, but then got stuck. Her attempt to free herself caused the door to give way, and she finally entered wearing the gate around her neck like a collar. I freed her at once but she seemed restless and in need of reassurance, for she sucked my thumb frantically.

During the following days Elsa shared her time between her mate and me. On our last night in camp Elsa made a terrific meal of goat and then, very heavy in the belly, went to join her lion, who had been calling for her for many hours. Her absence gave us an excellent opportunity to leave for Isiolo.

It was the hottest time of year, and there was a severe drought. The tribesmen, who in general avoided the region around Elsa's camp because it is infested with a type of tsetse fly which is fatal to domestic stock, now offered to pay in order to be allowed to bring their flocks into the reserve. The District Commissioner and George had several meetings with them and did their best to provide a solution to their problem, but, in spite of this, trespassing and poaching increased.

In the second week of November we were on our way back to Elsa. When we got near her lie-up we found the spoor of many sheep and goats. The campsite itself was patterned with hoofmarks. I trembled to think what might have happened to her should she have killed one of the tribesmen's goats which had been grazing in what she regarded as her private domain.

George sent a patrol of Game Scouts to deal with the poachers while he and I went out to look for Elsa. For some hours we walked through the bush, calling to her and at intervals shooting into the air, but there was no response. After dark a lion began to call from the direction of the Big Rock, but we listened in vain for Elsa's voice.

We had run out of "thunder flashes." When it became dark, we let her know we were there by turning on the air-raid siren, a relic of Mau-Mau days. In the past its penetrating howl had often brought her into camp.

It was answered by the lion. We sounded it again, and again he replied, and this strange conversation went on until it was interrupted by Elsa's arrival. She knocked us all over. As her body was wet, we realized that she must have swum across the river; she had come from the opposite direction to that from which the lion was calling.

She seemed very fit and was not hungry. She left at dawn, but returned at teatime when we were setting out for our walk. We climbed up the Big Rock and sat there watching the sun sink like a fireball behind the indigo hills.

Soon we had to return to camp, to the safety of our thorn enclosure and the lamps and rifles with which we armed ourselves against those dark hours in which Elsa's real life began. This was the moment at which we parted, each to return to his own world.

When we got back we found that there were a number of Boran poachers in camp who had been rounded up by the Game Scouts. As a Senior Game Warden, one of

George's most important tasks is to put down poaching, for it threatens the survival of wild life in the reserves.

Elsa kept away during that night and the following day. This worried us, as we would rather have had her under our eyes while so many tribesmen and their flocks were around. In the afternoon we went to look for her. As I came near to the rock, I called out to warn her of our approach and got no reply. But when we climbed onto the saddle of the rock where we had sat on the previous evening, we suddenly heard an alarming growl, followed by crashes and the sound of wood breaking inside the big cleft below us. We rushed to the top of the nearest rock; then we heard Elsa's voice very close and saw her lion making away swiftly through the bush. Elsa looked up at us, paused, and silently rushed after her mate.

George went back to Isiolo with the prisoners, but he left some Game Scouts in camp. The bush was full of sheep and goats which had straggled away from the flocks, and several newly born lambs were bleating piteously. With the help of the Scouts I found them and returned them to their mothers.

The evening was lit by lightning, a sure sign that the rains would start soon. Never had I greeted the first downpour with such a sense of relief. For this drenching meant that the Boran would return to their pastures, and temptation and danger would be removed from Elsa's path.

Fortunately, she did not like the crowd of Game Scouts who now shared our camp, so she spent these last dangerous days on the far side of the river, where there were neither Boran nor flocks.

When George returned he brought a zebra for Elsa. This was a special treat. As soon as she heard the vibra-

15

tions of the car, she appeared, spotted the kill, and tried to pull the carcass out of the Land Rover. Then, finding it too heavy for her, she walked over to where the boys were standing and, jerking her head at the zebra, made it plain that she needed help. They hauled the heavy animal a short distance amid much laughter, and then waited for Elsa to start her meal. To our astonishment, although zebra was her favorite meat, she did not eat, but stood by the river roaring in her loudest voice.

We presumed that she was inviting her mate to join in the feast. This would have been good lion manners. In the wild, the lionesses of the prides[1] do most of the killing, but they then have to wait to eat until the lion has had his fill.

The next morning, November 22, Elsa swam across the heavily flooded river, came up to the zebra, and roared repeatedly in the direction of the rocky range which is on our side of the river. Then, after she had eaten as much as she could, she went off toward the rocks.

For several days she divided her time between us and her lion.

When George returned from a patrol, he brought Elsa a goat. Usually she dragged her kill into his tent, presumably to avoid the trouble of having to guard it, but this time she left it lying beside the car, in a spot which could not be seen from the tent. During the night her mate came and had a good feed; we wondered whether this was what she had intended.

Next evening we took the precaution of placing some meat at a certain distance from the camp, for we did not want to encourage him to come too close.

Soon after dark we heard him dragging it away, and in the morning Elsa joined him.

[1] A pride is a company of lions in their wild state.

We were now faced with a problem. We wanted to help Elsa, who was increasingly handicapped by her pregnancy, by providing her with regular food, but we did not wish to interfere with her relations with her mate, by our continued presence in camp. But during the next six months, though we did not see him, we often heard his characteristic ten or twelve whuffing grunts and recognized his spoor, which proved that he remained Elsa's constant companion.

Though he still kept out of our sight, he had become bolder and bolder, and an extraordinary kind of truce seemed established between us. He had come to know our routine as intimately as we had come to know his habits. He shared Elsa's company with us, and we thought that in return he could fairly expect an occasional meal as compensation.

In the afternoon of December 1, Elsa came back and accompanied us when we walked to a rain pool; there she lay at the water's edge while I sat next to her and killed the tsetse flies which, in the failing light, were beginning to bite. While doing so, I read the "bush newspaper" in terms of the freshly imprinted spoor which surrounded the pool.

Suddenly I heard George give a whistle and, looking up, saw a herd of some twenty buffalo cows, many of them followed by calves, making their way to the water.

Elsa stared at the herd, raised herself very cautiously to a crouching position with her head on her paws, and then suddenly rushed at top speed toward the herd. There was a thundering noise and the crash of breaking wood as the buffaloes bolted, with Elsa in hot pursuit.

We ran after her and found her facing a thicket, panting hard. From within the bush came the angry snorting of the buffaloes. They had evidently rallied and were preparing to defend their young. A moment later several enraged cows charged Elsa, who, recognizing her limitations, withdrew, keeping in line with George, myself, and Makedde. Then she made a series of quick thrusts forward, but returned equally fast to her support.

George waited until the herd was within about fifteen yards of us, then he and Makedde shouted and each waved one arm, holding his rifle in the other. The animals were puzzled by this strange performance, and after a moment of indecision turned and made off. After a while we followed, but we took good care to make certain that no buffalo was waiting to ambush us, for they are notoriously dangerous creatures.

Next morning George had to leave. I stayed on, and Elsa spent three days in camp with me in spite of the continual calling of her mate.

One evening she looked toward the river, stiffened, and then rushed into the bush. A tremendous barking of baboons ensued, till it was silenced by her roars. Soon she was answered by her lion — he must have been only about fifty yards away. His voice seemed to shake the earth, and it increased in strength. From the other side Elsa roared back. Sitting between them, I became a little anxious in case the loving pair should decide to come into my tent. However, in time they appeared to have roared themselves hoarse. Their whuffings died away and no further sound came from the bush.

Elsa in her own world.

The Birth of the Cubs

IT was now nearly mid-December, and we believed that the cubs might arrive at any moment.

Elsa was so heavy that every movement seemed to require an effort; if she had been living a normal life, she would certainly have taken exercise, so I did my best to make her go for walks with me, but she kept close to the tents. We wondered what place she would choose for her delivery, and even thought that since she had always considered our tent as her safest "den," the cubs might be born in it.

The river was now in flood, and George and I decided to walk three miles downstream to look at some cataracts,[1] which are very impressive when the water is high. Elsa watched our departure from the top of the Land Rover. She made no attempt to join us and looked sleepy.

[1] Waterfalls.

On our way back, as soon as I was out of earshot of the cataracts, I heard Elsa's familiar *hnk-hnk* and soon saw her trotting along the path as quickly as she could to join us. I was very touched, the more so that, though her lion had roared desperately for her during the whole of the previous night, she had made no attempt to join him.

This was very gratifying, but it also reminded us of our fear that her lion might get tired of sharing her with us. It had taken us a very long time to find a mate for her; it would be unforgivable if our interference now caused him to leave her. We wanted her cubs to grow up as wild lions, and to do this they needed their father. We decided to go away for three days.

We returned on December 16 and found a very hungry Elsa waiting for us. For two days she remained in camp; possibly frequent thunderstorms made her reluctant to leave its shelter. She did, however, take a few short walks — always to the Big Rock — but returned quickly. She ate unbelievably, and we felt that she was stocking up a reserve for the days that lay ahead.

On the night of December 18 she crept in the dark through the thorn fence which surrounded my tent and spent the night close to my bed. This was something which she had very rarely done since her release, and I took it as a sign that she felt her time was near.

The next day when George and I went for a walk, Elsa followed us, but she had to sit down at intervals, panting and plainly in great discomfort. When we saw this we turned back and walked very slowly. Suddenly she turned off into the bush in the direction of the Big Rock.

She did not return during that night, but in the morning we heard her calling in a very weak voice. We thought this might mean that she had had her cubs and went out to trace her spoor. These led us close to the rock, but the grass was so high that we lost track of her. The rock range is about a mile long, and though we searched for a long time we could not discover where she was.

We set out again in the afternoon and eventually we spotted her through our field glasses. She was standing on the Big Rock.

We climbed up and found her lying close to a large boulder which stood at the top of a wide cleft in the rock. Near to it there was some grass, and a small tree provided shade. This place had always been one of Elsa's favorite "lookouts," and we felt that it would make an ideal nursery, since inside the cleft was a rainproof and well-protected cave.

We left her to take the initiative, and presently she came slowly toward us, walking very carefully and obviously in pain. She greeted us very affectionately, then went over to Makedde and the Toto, who had remained behind, and rubbed her head against their legs before she sat down.

When I came near her she got up and moved to the edge of the rock, and remained there with her head turned away from us. It seemed to me that she chose this precipitous position to make sure that no one could follow her. At intervals she came back and rubbed her head very gently against mine, and then walked determinedly back to the boulder, making it plain that she wished to be left alone.

We went a short distance away, and for half an hour watched her through our field glasses. She rolled from side to side and moaned repeatedly. Suddenly she rose, went very carefully down the steep rock face, and disappeared into the thick bush at its base.

Since there was nothing we could do to help her, we went back to camp. After dark we heard her lion calling; there was no reply.

I lay awake most of the night thinking about her, and when toward morning it started to rain, my anxiety increased.

Very early, George and I set out. First we followed the spoor of Elsa's lion. He had been close to the camp, had dragged off the very smelly carcass of the goat which Elsa had not touched for three days, and had eaten it in the bush. Then he had walked to the rock near the place where we had seen Elsa disappear.

We wondered what we should do next. We did not want our curiosity to bring any risk to the cubs — captive lionesses who have been disturbed soon after giving birth to cubs have been known to kill their young. We also thought that her lion might be very near, so we decided to stop our search. Instead, George went off and shot a large waterbuck to provide Elsa and her mate with plenty of food.

We took up the lion's tracks where we had left them, and traced them till they reached a dry watercourse near the rock. There we left his meal, thinking that if he came for it, this might help us to find Elsa.

During the night we heard him roaring in the distance, and were therefore surprised next morning to find his pugmarks close to the camp. He had not taken any of the meat that was close to the camp, however, but had gone to the kill we had left for him near the rock. This he had dragged for at least half a mile through most difficult terrain, across ravines, rocky outcrops, and dense bush.

After breakfast we went out again; through our field glasses we saw a great flock of vultures perched on the trees near the spot where we thought the lion had made his meal.

Assuming he had finished by now, we approached the place. Every bush and tree was loaded with birds of prey, all staring at the dry watercourse where the carcass was lying. Since the meat was in the open, and yet the vultures did not leave their perches, we concluded that the lion was guarding his kill. As far as we could see he had not touched it, so we thought that Elsa too might be close by and that her gallant mate had dragged the four-hundred-pound waterbuck this long distance for her benefit.

We went back to camp for lunch, after which we set out again. When we saw that the vultures were still on the trees, we circled the place upwind and approached it very cautiously from the high ground.

George, Makedde, and I had just passed a very thick bush which overhung a deep crack in the ground when I suddenly had a strange, uncomfortable feeling. I stopped and, looking back, saw the Toto, who was close behind me, staring intently at the bush. Next there was a terrifying growl and the sound of snapping branches; a second later all was quiet again — the lion had gone. We had passed within six feet of him. I think he had been watching our movements with great intensity, and when the

Toto stooped to see what was in the bush, the lion couldn't stand it and went off. They had actually looked straight into each other's eyes, and the Toto had seen his big body disappear into the deep crack.

It was now four days since we had seen Elsa, and six since she had eaten anything — unless she had shared the waterbuck with her mate.

We believed that she had given birth to the cubs on the night of December 20. It could not be a coincidence that her lion, who had not been about for days, had reappeared on that night and remained close to the rock ever since.

On Christmas Eve, George went to get a goat while I continued the fruitless search and called to Elsa without getting any answer.

It was with a heavy heart that I prepared our little Christmas tree. In the past I had always improvised one. But tonight I had a real little tree complete with glittering tinsel branches, sparkling decorations, and candles. I placed it on a table outside the tents, which I had covered with flowers and greenery. Then I collected the presents which I had brought for George, Makedde, Nuru, Ibrahim, the Toto, and the cook, and the sealed envelopes containing money for the boys on which I had painted a Christmas-tree branch. There were also packages of cigarettes and dates and cans of milk for them.

I changed quickly into a dress, and by then it was dark enough to light the candles. I called the men, who came dressed up for the occasion, grinning but a little shy, for never before had they seen a Christmas tree of this kind.

I must admit to having been deeply moved, myself,

when I saw the little silver tree sparkling in the vast darkness of the surrounding bush, bringing the message of the birth of Christ.

On Christmas Eve I always feel like a small child. To break the tension, I told the men about the European custom of celebrating Christmas Eve with a tree. After I had given them their presents, we all gave three cheers for "Elsa, Elsa, Elsa." The sound seemed to hang on the air, and I felt a lump rise in my throat — was she alive?

Quickly I told the cook to bring in the plum pudding which we had brought from Isiolo, and then to pour brandy over it and light it. But no bluish flame arose, for our Christmas pudding was a soggy mass which had a distinct smell of Worcestershire sauce. Certainly the cook had never before been in charge of such a ritual. He had paid no attention to my instructions and had remained fixed in his belief that George loved his Worcestershire sauce so much, it must be appropriate to souse even the plum pudding with it.

We were not, however, the only ones to be disappointed in our Christmas dinner. We had hung a goat carcass out of the reach of predators, which we would lower if Elsa appeared. After we had gone to bed we heard her lion grunting and growling by the tree and performing all sorts of acrobatics. He went on for a long time and then retired exhausted.

Early on Christmas morning we went in search of Elsa. After hours of fruitless tracking we came back for breakfast, and during the morning George shot at an aggressive cobra which we found close to the camp.

Later we set out once more for the rocky range. Something seemed to tell us that if Elsa were still alive, that was where she would be. We wiggled through dense bush, and I crept hopefully into every crevice. When we were all tired out we sat down to rest in the shade of an overhanging rock and discussed every possible fate which might have overtaken Elsa.

We tried to cheer ourselves up by quoting cases of dogs who would not leave their litters for the first five or six days because they had to keep their pups warm, feed them, and massage their bellies to help their digestive functions to start working. Indeed, we had expected Elsa to have a similar reaction, but this did not account for the absence of *any* trace of her.

At midday we returned to camp and began a very gloomy and silent Christmas meal.

Suddenly there was a swift movement, and before I could take in what was happening, Elsa was between us, sweeping everything off the table, knocking us to the ground, sitting on us, and overwhelming us with joy and affection.

Her figure was normal again; she looked superbly fit.

We gave her some meat, which she immediately ate. Meanwhile, we discussed many questions. Why had she come to visit us during the hottest part of the day, a time when normally she would never move? Could it be that she had chosen it deliberately because it was the safest time to leave the cubs, since few predators would be on the prowl in such heat? Or had she heard the shot which George had fired at the cobra, and had she taken it as a signal to her? Why were her teats small and dry? Had she just suckled the cubs? But this would not seem to explain why her milk glands, which had been so big during her pregnancy, had now shrunk to their normal size. Had the cubs died? And why had she waited for five days before coming to us for food?

After she had had a good meal and drunk some water she rubbed her head affectionately against us, walked about thirty yards down the river, and lay down and dozed. We left her alone, so that she should feel at ease. When I looked for her at teatime, she had gone.

Next day we began to worry about the cubs. If they were alive, was their mother able to suckle them? We were very anxious because we had been warned by zoo authorities that hand-reared lionesses often produce abnormal cubs which do not live. We felt we just *must* know about the cubs and rescue them if necessary.

The next morning we searched for five hours, but we did not find Elsa's nursery. We carried on equally unsuccessfully in the afternoon. While plodding through the bush, George nearly stepped on an exceptionally large puff adder and was lucky to shoot it before it could strike.

Half an hour later we heard Ibrahim popping off a gun, a signal that Elsa had arrived in camp. Obviously she had responded to the shot with which George had dispatched the puff adder.

She was most affectionate to us when we got back, but Ibrahim told us that her behavior had been very unusual. When he fetched the gun from the kitchen, which was in the direction from which she had come, she dashed angrily at him. Possibly she thought he was going to her cubs. Later, when he went to collect her meat which was hanging by the river in the shade, she prevented him from touching her kill.

Now, having eaten enormously, Elsa settled down and showed no intention of returning to her cubs. This alarmed me because it was getting dark; it was the worst moment to leave them alone.

We tried to induce her to return to them by walking along the path down which she had come. She followed us reluctantly, listening alertly in the direction of the rock, but soon returned to camp and went back to her meal. It was only after she had methodically cleaned up every scrap of it that she disappeared into the dark. Had she waited till there was no light, to make sure we could not follow her?

We were now convinced that she was looking after her cubs. But after the warnings we had had from the zoo experts, we could not be happy until we had seen for ourselves that they were normal.

Very early in the morning we set out and followed Elsa's spoor, which led toward the Big Rock. Close to it was what seemed to us an ideal home for a lioness and her family. Large boulders gave complete shelter, and they were surrounded by bush that was almost impenetrable. We made straight for the topmost boulder, and from it tried to look down into the center of the "den." We saw no pugmarks, but there were signs that some animal had used it as a lie-up.

After we had called loudly for half an hour, Elsa suddenly appeared out of a cluster of bush only twenty yards away. She seemed rather shocked at seeing us, stared, and kept silent and very still.

Perhaps we were so close to her nursery that she had thought it better to appear and so prevent us from finding it. After a few moments, she walked up to us and was very affectionate to George, myself, Makedde, and the Toto, but she never uttered a sound. To my relief I saw that her teats were twice their normal length and that the hair around them was still wet from suckling her cubs.

Soon she went slowly back toward the bush, and for about five minutes stood with her back turned toward us, listening intently for any sound from the thicket. Then she sat down, still with her back turned to us. It was as though she wanted to say to us, "Here my private world begins, and you must not trespass."

It was a dignified demonstration, and no words could have conveyed her wishes more clearly. We sneaked away as quietly as we could, making a detour in order to climb to the top of the Big Rock. From it we looked down and saw her sitting just as we had left her. Obviously she had got our scent, knew just what we were doing, and did not intend to let us discover her lie-up.

This made me realize how unaware we had been, in spite of our intimacy with Elsa, of the reactions of wild animals. It amused me to remember how we had prepared ourselves against the possibility of the cubs' being born in our tent, and how we had flattered ourselves that Elsa regarded it as the place in which she felt safest.

Although the spoor we had recently found had all led toward the lower rock, we thought it possible that the cubs had been born in the boulder hide-out and that later Elsa had moved them about thirty yards to where they now were. She had probably made the move after the rains stopped, for while the boulder lie-up was rainproof, the new one was not, though otherwise it was an ideal nursery.

I determined to stay on in camp in order to provide her with food, so that she would have no need to leave her family unguarded for long periods while she went out hunting for them. We also decided to take her meals to her, to reduce the time she would have to desert the cubs.

We put our plan into immediate operation and that afternoon went by car, close to her lie-up. We knew that Elsa would associate the vibrations of the engine with us and with food. As we neared the place where we had last seen her, we started to call out, *"Maji, chakula, nyama"* — Swahili words meaning "water," "food," "meat," with which Elsa was familiar.

Soon she came, was as affectionate as usual, and ate a lot. While she had her head in a basin which we had sunk in the ground to keep it steady, and was busy drinking, we went off. She looked around when she heard the engine start, but made no move to follow us.

Later the next day George went off to Isiolo. Elsa stayed in camp with me till the late afternoon; then I saw her sneak into the bush upstream, and I followed her. Obviously she did not wish to be observed, for when she caught my scent, she pretended to sharpen her claws on a tree. Then as soon as I turned my back on her, she jumped at me and knocked me over, as though to say, "That's for spying on me!"

Now it was my turn to pretend — that I had only come to bring more meat to her. She accepted my excuse, followed me, and began eating again. After this, nothing would induce her to return to the cubs until long after night had fallen; I was reading in my tent then, and she felt certain that I would not be likely to follow her.

One afternoon when I was passing the Big Rock I saw a

very strange animal standing on it. In the dim light it looked like a cross between a hyena and a small lion. When it saw me it sneaked off with the gait of a cat. It had obviously spotted the cubs, and I was much alarmed.

Later, I drove up with some food. Elsa came at once when I called her; she seemed unusually alert and was rather fierce to the Toto. I left her still eating on the roof of my truck. It was there that we placed the meat in the evening, to keep it out of the reach of predators; few of them would risk jumping onto this unknown object, even if they were capable of doing so.

I did not know what to do for the best. If I continued to leave food close to Elsa's nursery, would it not attract predators? But if I kept the meat in camp and Elsa had to desert her cubs to come and fetch it, might they not be killed while she was absent? Faced with these two unsatisfactory choices, I decided to go on providing food near her lie-up.

I also made up my mind that, in spite of her disapproval, I had better find out how many cubs there were and whether they were all right. I might then be able to help in an emergency.

On January 11, I did an unpardonable thing. Accompanied by the Toto, whom Elsa knew well, I climbed the rock face, calling repeatedly to warn her of our approach. She did not answer. I told the Toto to take off his sandals so as not to make any noise.

When we had reached the top, we stood on the edge of the cliff and raked the bush below with our field glasses. Immediately under us was the place from which Elsa had emerged that first time, when we had surprised her and she had stood on guard.

"Elsa settled down and showed no intention of returning to her cubs."

Now there was no sign of her, although the place looked like a well-used nursery.

I was concentrating very hard on the bush below us, but suddenly I had a strange feeling. I dropped my field glasses, turned, and saw Elsa creeping up behind the Toto. I had just time to shout a warning to him before she knocked him down. She had crept up the rock behind us quite silently. The Toto only missed toppling over the cliff by a hair's breadth, and that mainly because his feet were bare, which gave him the chance of getting a grip on the rock.

Next Elsa walked over to me and knocked me over in a friendly way, but it was very obvious that she was expressing annoyance at finding us so close to her cubs.

After this demonstration she walked slowly along the crest of the rock, from time to time looking back over her shoulder to make sure we were following her. Silently she led us to the far end of the ridge. There we climbed down into the bush. As soon as we were on level ground she rushed ahead, repeatedly turning her head back to make sure that we were coming.

In this way she took us back to the road, but she made a wide detour, presumably to avoid passing near the cubs. I interpreted her complete silence as a wish not to alarm them or to prevent them from emerging and following us.

When we walk together I usually pat Elsa occasionally and she likes it, but today she would not allow me to touch her and made it clear that I was in disgrace. Even when she was eating her dinner on the roof of the car back in camp, whenever I came near her she turned away from me.

She did not go to the cubs until it was dark.

Elsa visits us at teatime.

We See the Cubs

GEORGE came up from Isiolo and we changed guard. Elsa had made me feel that I could do no more spying on her; but George had not had the same experience. So one afternoon, while I was in Isiolo a hundred and fifty miles away, George crept very quietly up Elsa's Big Rock and peered over the top.

Below he saw her suckling two cubs, and as her head was hidden by an overhanging rock, he felt sure she had not seen him.

Having seen the family, George went back to camp and collected a goat carcass. This he deposited near the nursery, but Elsa did not come to fetch the meat. This made him feel guilty. Had she refused to go near the kill because she was aware that George had spied on her? When, during the following day she failed to come to camp, George feared this. However, at nightfall she arrived and was ravenously hungry.

I did not return from Isiolo till a few days later, having picked up a new supply of goats *en route*. How thrilled I was to hear the good news!

George had had only a brief sight of the two suckling cubs — not time to discover whether they were normal. And of course he could not tell whether there might be others hidden from his view. So on the afternoon of January 14, when Elsa was in camp feeding, he crept off to the Zom Rocks while I kept her company.

For two days she had been constantly in this area, so we supposed she had changed the place of the nursery.

George climbed up to the top of the center rock and inside a cleft saw three cubs: two were asleep, and the third was chewing at some sansevieria.[1] The cub looked up at him, but as its eyes were still blurred and bluish, he did not think that it could focus well enough to see him. Then the two cubs who had been sleeping woke up and crawled about. It seemed to him that they were perfectly healthy.

When he came back to camp and told me the excellent news, Elsa was still there and quite unsuspicious.

At dusk we drove her near to the Zom Rocks. But only after we had tactfully walked away, and she was reassured by hearing our voices fading into the distance, did she jump off the Land Rover, presumably to join the cubs.

On February 2, while I was writing in the studio, the Toto came running to tell me that Elsa was calling in a very strange voice from the other side of the river. I went upstream, following the sound, till I broke through the undergrowth at a place close to our camp. There, in the

[1] A tropical plant of the lily family.

dry season, is a fairly wide sandbank on our side, and on the other a dry watercourse which drops abruptly into the river.

Suddenly I stopped, unable to believe my eyes.

There was Elsa standing on the sandbank within a few yards of me, one cub close to her, a second cub emerging from the water shaking itself dry, and the third one still on the far bank, pacing to and fro and calling piteously. Elsa looked fixedly at me, her expression a mixture of pride and embarrassment.

I remained absolutely still while she gave a gentle moan to her young that sounded like *"m-hm, m-hm"*; then she walked up to the landing cub, licked it affectionately, and turned back to the river to go to the youngster who was stranded on the far bank. The two cubs who had come across with her followed her immediately, swimming bravely through the deep water, and soon the family was reunited.

They landed near a fig tree. Elsa rested in its shade, her golden coat showing up vividly against the dark-green foliage and the silver-gray boulders. At first the cubs hid, but soon their curiosity got the better of their shyness. They began by peeping cautiously at me through the undergrowth, and then came out into the open and stared inquisitively.

Elsa *m-hm, m-hm'*d, which reassured them, and when they were quite at their ease they began to climb onto their mother's back and tried to catch her switching tail. Rolling affectionately over her, exploring the rocks, and squeezing their fat little tummies under the roots of the fig tree, they forgot all about me.

After a while Elsa rose and went to the water's edge, intending to enter the river again; one cub was close to her and plainly meant to follow her.

Unfortunately, at this moment the Toto, whom I had sent back to fetch Elsa's food, arrived with it. Immediately Elsa flattened her ears and remained immobile until the boy had dropped the meat and gone away. Then she swam quickly across, followed by one cub, which kept close to her, although it seemed to be quite unafraid of the water. When Elsa settled down to her meal the plucky little fellow turned back and started to swim over on its own to join, or perhaps to help, the other two cubs.

As soon as Elsa saw it swimming out of its depth, she plunged into the river, caught up with it, grabbed its head in her mouth, and ducked it so thoroughly that I was quite worried about the little chap.

When she had given it a lesson not to be too venturesome, she retrieved it and brought it, dangling out of her mouth, to our bank.

By this time a second cub plucked up courage and swam across, its tiny head just visible above the rippling water, but the third cub stayed on the far bank looking frightened.

Elsa came up to me and began rolling on her back and showing her affection for me. It seemed as though she wanted to prove to her cubs that I was part of the pride and could be trusted.

Reassured, the two cubs crept cautiously closer and closer, their large expressive eyes watching Elsa's every movement and mine, till they were within three feet of me. I found it difficult to restrain an impulse to lean forward and touch them, but I remembered the warning a zoologist had given me: "Never touch cubs unless they take the initiative." This three-foot limit seemed to be an invisible boundary which they felt they must not cross.

While all this was happening, the third cub kept up a pathetic miaowing from the far bank, appealing for help.

Elsa watched it for a time; then she walked to the water's edge, at the point at which the river is narrowest. With the two brave cubs cuddling beside her, she called to the timid one to join them. But its only response was to pace nervously up and down; it was too frightened to try to cross.

When Elsa saw it so distressed she went to its rescue, accompanied by the two bold ones, who seemed to enjoy swimming.

Soon they were all on the opposite side again, where they had a wonderful time climbing up the steep bank of a sand *lugga*[1] which runs into the river, rolling down it, landing on each other's backs, and balancing on the trunk of a fallen doum palm.

Elsa licked them affectionately, talked to them in her soft moaning voice, never let them out of her sight, and whenever one ventured too far off for her liking, went after the explorer and brought it back.

I watched them for about an hour and then called Elsa, who replied in her usual voice, which was quite different from the one she used when talking to the cubs.

She came down to the water's edge, waited till all her family were at her feet, and started to swim across. This time all three cubs came with her.

As soon as they had landed, she licked each one in turn and then, instead of charging up to me as she usually does

[1] Dry riverbed.

when coming out of the river, she walked up slowly, rubbed herself gently against me, rolled in the sand, licked my face, and finally hugged me. I was very much moved by her obvious wish to show her cubs that we were friends. They watched us from a distance, interested but puzzled, and determined to stay out of reach.

Next, Elsa and the cubs went to the carcass, which she started eating, while the youngsters licked the skin and tore at it, somersaulted over it, and became very excited. It was probably their first encounter with a kill.

The evidence suggested that they were six weeks and two days old. They were in excellent condition, and though they still had a bluish film over their eyes, they could certainly see perfectly. Their coats had fewer spots than Elsa's or her sisters', and were also much less thick than theirs had been at the same age, but far finer and more shiny. I could not tell their sex, but I noticed immediately that the cub with the lightest coat was much livelier and more inquisitive than the other two, and especially devoted to its mother. It always cuddled close up to her, if possible under her chin, and embraced her with its little paws. Elsa was very gentle and patient with her family, and allowed them to crawl all over her and chew her ears and tail.

Gradually she moved closer to me and seemed to be inviting me to join in their game. But when I wiggled my fingers in the sand, the cubs cocked their round foxy faces but kept their distance.

When it got dark, Elsa listened attentively and then took the cubs some yards into the bush. A few moments later I heard the sound of suckling.

I returned to camp, and when I arrived it was wonderful to find Elsa and the cubs waiting for me about ten yards from the tent.

I patted her, and she licked my hand. Then I called the Toto, and together we brought the remains of the carcass up from the river. Elsa watched us, and it seemed to me she was pleased that we were relieving her of the task of pulling the heavy load. But when we came within twenty yards of her, she suddenly rushed at us with flattened ears. I told the boy to drop the meat and remain still, and I began to drag it near to the cubs.

When she saw that I was handling the kill alone, Elsa was reassured, and as soon as I deposited it she started eating. After watching her for a while, I went to my tent and was surprised to see her following me. She flung herself on the ground and called to the cubs to come and join me. But they remained outside miaowing; soon she went back to them and so did I.

We all sat together on the grass, Elsa leaning against me while she suckled her family.

Suddenly two of the cubs started quarreling over a teat. Elsa reacted by rolling into a position which gave them better access. In doing so she came to rest against me and hugged me with one paw, including me in her family.

So many people had warned me that after Elsa's cubs had been born she would probably turn into a fierce and dangerous mother defending her young; yet here she was as trusting and as affectionate as ever, and wanting me to share her happiness. I felt very humble.

Elsa was a gentle and patient mother.

One of the cubs at four and a half months.

The Cubs
Meet Friends

NEXT morning there was no sign of Elsa or the cubs, and as it had rained during the night all spoor had been washed away.

About teatime she turned up alone, very hungry. I held her meat while she chewed it, so as to keep her attention, and meanwhile told the Toto to follow her fresh pugmarks to get a clue to the present whereabouts of the cubs.

When he returned, Elsa hopped onto the roof of my car, and from this platform she watched the two of us walking back along her tracks into the bush.

I did this deliberately to induce her to return to the cubs. When she realized where we were going, she promptly followed us and, taking the lead, trotted quickly along her pugmarks; several times she waited till, panting, we caught up with her. I wondered whether at last she meant to take us to her lie-up.

When we reached the "Whuffing Rock" — where we had once surprised her with her mate and had been startled by their alarming whuffing — she stopped to listen. Then she climbed swiftly halfway up the slope, hesitated until I had caught up with her, and then rushed ahead till she had reached the saddle of the rock, where the big cleft breaks off on the far side. There, much out of breath, I joined her. I was about to pat her when she flattened her ears, and with an angry snarl gave me a heavy clout. Since it was plain that I was not wanted, I retreated. When I had gone halfway down the face of the rock, I looked back and saw Elsa playing with one cub, while another was emerging from the cleft.

I was puzzled at the sudden change in her behavior, but I respected her wishes and left her and her family alone. I joined the Toto, who had waited in the bush just below, and we watched Elsa through our field glasses. As soon as she saw that we were at a safe distance she relaxed, and the cubs came out and began playing with her. One cub was certainly much more attached to her than the others; it often sat between her front paws and rubbed its head against her chin, while the two others busily investigated their surroundings.

George returned on February 4, and was delighted to hear the good news of the cubs; in the afternoon we walked toward the Whuffing Rock, hoping that he too might see the cubs.

On our way we heard the agitated barking of baboons. We thought it very likely that Elsa's presence was the cause of the commotion, so, as we approached the river, we called out to her. She appeared immediately, but though she was very friendly she was obviously upset, and rushed nervously backward and forward between us and the bush, which grew along the river's edge. She seemed to be doing her best to prevent us from reaching the water.

We assumed that her cubs were there, and were surprised that she should try to prevent George from seeing them. In the end she led us back to the camp by a wide detour.

Two days later we saw her near the Whuffing Rock. As we were walking toward it we talked rather loudly, to give her notice of our approach. She emerged from the thick undergrowth at the mouth of the cleft and stood very still, gazing at us. After a few moments she sat down facing us — we were still some two hundred yards away — and made it very plain that we were not to come any nearer. Several times she turned her head toward the cleft and listened attentively, but apart from this she remained in her "guarding" position.

We now realized that she made a difference between bringing the cubs to see us and our visiting them.

Two weeks passed before she brought the cubs to camp to introduce them to George. This was not entirely her fault, for during this time we were obliged to go to Isiolo for a couple of days, and while we were away she and the cubs had arrived at the camp one morning looking for us, but had only found the boys.

Makedde told us that he had gone to meet her and she had rubbed her head against his legs, and one plucky cub had boldly walked up to within a short distance of him.

However, when he squatted and tried to pat it, it had

snarled and run off to join the others, who were hiding some distance away. They had stayed in camp till lunchtime and then left. Elsa returned alone during the afternoon asking for meat, but the goat carcass was by then very high and she left in disgust after dark.

I arrived about an hour after she had gone. Makedde was delighted with the plucky cub; he said he was sure it was a male and told me he had given it a name, which was, he said, very popular with the Meru tribe. It sounded like Jespah. I asked him and the other boys where the name came from. They said it was out of the Bible, but as each boy pronounced it slightly differently it was difficult for me to trace it. The nearest phonetic association I could find was Japhtah, which means, "God sets free." If that were the origin of the little cub's name, it could not be more appropriate. Later, when we knew that the family consisted of two lions and a lioness, we called Jespah's brother, who was very timid, Gopa, for in Swahili this means "timid," and his sister we named Little Elsa.

The following morning it was drizzling. I woke up to hear Elsa's typical cub moan coming from across the river and was just in time to see her crossing the river with her cubs. Jespah was close to her, the other two some distance behind.

She walked slowly up to me, licked me, and sat down next to me. Then she called repeatedly to the cubs. Jespah ventured fairly near to me, but the others kept their distance. I collected some meat, which Elsa promptly dragged into a nearby bush. She and the cubs spent the next two hours eating it, while I sat on a sandbank watching them.

While they ate, Elsa talked continuously to the cubs in a series of low moans. They often suckled, but also chewed at the meat; they were now about nine weeks old.

After a while I went off to have breakfast, and soon afterward saw Elsa leading the cubs in a wide circle to the car track. I followed slowly, hoping to take some photographs, but she stopped suddenly broadside across the road and flattened her ears. I accepted the reproof and went back, turned to have a last look at them and saw the cubs bouncing along behind their mother, going in the direction of the Big Rock. By now they were lively walkers, chasing and prodding one another as they tried to keep pace with Elsa. In spite of their high spirits they were most obedient to her call, and were also already well trained in cleanliness.

During the next few days Elsa often came alone to visit us. She was always affectionate, but some of her habits had altered since she had given birth to the cubs. She now very seldom ambushed us, was less playful and more dignified.

On February 19 George came "on duty," while I returned to Isiolo. I was to meet Lord William Percy and his wife, and bring them back to see Elsa's family. In general we discouraged visitors, but these old friends had known Elsa since she was a cub; they had always shown the greatest interest in her.

On our arrival in camp, George told us that he had finally seen the cubs. He said that Elsa had been about to cross to our side of the river with her cubs, but when she became aware of our car approaching, she had retired into the bush.

Soon she emerged, but seemed nervous and disinclined to enter the water. To induce her to join us I called to her and placed a carcass close to the river.

She made no move till I had gone back to our friends. Then she swam quickly across, seized the goat, and rushed back with it to the cubs. Once across, she dragged it onto a grassy patch, where the whole family set to and had a good meal.

After it had grown dark we heard fearful growls, and by the light of our torches saw Elsa defending her kill from a crocodile, which, when it observed us, disappeared quickly into the water. Next morning the spoor showed that in the end the "croc" had been successful in stealing the carcass.

Elsa always seemed to know just how far she could go with these reptiles. She had never shown any fear of them, although we knew that in this river there were many crocodiles measuring twelve feet or more. She had her favorite crossings and avoided the places where the river was very deep, and besides taking this precaution there can be no doubt that she had some means of sensing the presence of crocs. How this worked we could not guess. We had our own method of discovering the presence of crocs; we knew that they invariably respond to a certain sound, which can roughly be represented by "*imn, imn, imn,*" and we often took advantage of our knowledge.

Next day, while we were having tea in the studio, Elsa appeared alone; our friends were included in her customary friendly rubbings, and she bore with my taking a few photographs, but then walked out of the picture.

Later Lady William started sketching her. I kept close

by in case Elsa might suddenly take a dislike to serving as a model. However, she appeared quite indifferent to what was going on, and after a while I went away. As soon as my back was turned she rushed like lightning at the artist and embraced her playfully. As Elsa weighs about three hundred pounds, I admired the calm way in which Lady William accepted the demonstration. After this, we decided that the sketching had better cease.

At teatime the next day we saw Elsa and the cubs on the opposite side of the river. Later, they all got thirsty and came to the water's edge to drink. I was glad that our guests should have this splendid view of them drinking close together, their heads stretched forward between the pointed elbows of their front legs, which were bent. At first they just lapped noisily; then they plunged into the shallow water and began to play. A big boulder surrounded by water made a perfect setting for playing "king of the castle," and I thought of the days when Elsa and her sisters had had to be content with a potato bag on our veranda at Isiolo for their "castle."

After our friends had gone to bed, George and I returned to see Elsa. We found her standing at the water's edge facing a crocodile, whose head rose out of the river about four feet away.

We did not want to frighten the cubs by firing a shot, so I tempted Elsa to leave the place by offering her a treat of which she was very fond; it consists of brains, marrow, calcium, and cod-liver oil. I began giving it to her when she was pregnant, and she found it irresistible.

Now she followed the bowl in which I carried it and

came with the cubs to sit in front of our tent, facing the bright lamplight. The cubs were unperturbed by the glare; perhaps they thought it was a new kind of moon.

Early one morning Elsa visited the camp before anyone was up. I heard her and followed her. She was already in the water when I called to her, but she came back at once, settled with me on a sandbank, and began to miaow at the cubs, encouraging them to come near us. They approached within three yards, but obviously did not wish to be handled; and as the last thing I wanted was that they should become tame, I was very pleased about this. Elsa seemed puzzled that they should still be scared of me, but in the end she gave up her attempt to make us fraternize, took her family across the river, and disappeared into the bush.

At ten o'clock she returned alone, sniffed restlessly in the river bush, and then trotted, scenting, along the road she had taken in the morning.

After we had lost sight of her, we heard her growling fiercely. She returned along the track still sniffing anxiously, and finally roared at full strength toward the rock, after which she rushed into the river and disappeared into the bush on the far side. We did not know to what to attribute her strange behavior; we thought perhaps she might have lost a cub.

At lunchtime Ibrahim brought in three tribesmen who said they were looking for a goat which had strayed; but as they carried bows and arrows, we felt sure that we had been right. No doubt their arrival had startled the little ones and they had bolted.

Elsa did not bring the cubs into camp again for a couple of days. Then one morning we took our friends to see the magnificent falls of the Tana River, and on our return we found Elsa and the cubs in camp.

Later, we had our supper while they enjoyed their dinner. We were silent, for we knew how sensitive the cubs were to the sound of talking. They did not mind the chatter of the boys, far away in the kitchen; but if we were near them and said a word to each other, even in a low voice, they sneaked away. As for the clicking of a camera shutter, it gave them the jitters.

The cubs were ten weeks old and Elsa had begun to wean them. Whenever she thought they had had enough milk, she either sat on her teats or jumped onto the roof of the Land Rover. So if the cubs did not want to starve, they had to eat meat. They tore the intestines of the kills out of their mother's mouth and sucked them in like spaghetti, through closed teeth, pressing out the unwanted contents, just as she did.

That evening one cub was determined to get some more milk, and persistently pushed its way under Elsa's belly until she became really angry, gave it a good cuff, and jumped onto the car.

The little ones resented this very much; they stood on their hind legs resting their forepaws against the car, miaowing up at their mother, but she sat and licked her paws, as though she were quite unaware of the whimpering cubs below.

When they had recovered from their disappointment they bounced off, cheerfully making explorations which took them out of her sight. Elsa became extremely alert.

She called them, and when they did not reappear quickly, she hopped off the car and fetched them back to safety.

The next two evenings Elsa came to camp without her family. She was exuberantly affectionate to all of us and swept the table clear of our supper, which made our friends appreciate why in camp we use crockery and glasses made of unbreakable material. On the third evening she brought the cubs with her and behaved in the same way. We were rather surprised to observe that the cubs were not in the least startled when our supper landed on the ground with a noisy clatter.

During all that night it poured without stopping, and the next day I went off to Isiolo with our friends. George stayed on in camp. We knew that once the rains started in earnest, transport would soon become very difficult.

The cubs cross the river with Elsa.

The Cubs in Camp

I CAME back to camp two days later to relieve George. For several nights we had terrific thunderstorms, and the lightning and the crashes came so close together that I was quite frightened. The water poured down as though it were flowing through a pipe.

As George's tent was empty, Elsa and the cubs could very well have sheltered in it, but the youngsters' inbred fear of man was so great that they preferred to get soaked outside. This trait was the most obvious sign of their wild blood, and it was something we were determined to encourage, even at the expense of a wetting and even in defiance of Elsa's wish to make them into friends of ours. Often she seemed to be playing a sort of "catch as catch can" with them, circling nearer and nearer to the tent in which I was sitting, as though she wanted to bring them into it without their realizing what was happening.

Twice she dashed into the tent and, peeping over my shoulder, called to them. But they never overstepped their self-imposed frontier. It seemed that our rearing of their mother in domesticity had in no way impaired the instinct which all wild animals possess and which warns them against approaching an unknown danger. Moreover, by concealing her cubs from us for five or six weeks, Elsa herself had shown that her own instinct for protecting her young was still alive.

And yet Elsa seemed plainly disappointed that her efforts to make one pride of us were proving unsuccessful. One evening she entered my tent, deliberately lay down behind me, and then called softly to the cubs, inviting them to suckle her. By doing this she tried not only to make the cubs come into the tent but also to force them to pass close to me. No doubt they would have been pleased if I had retired behind their mother, and she would have been pleased if I had done something to encourage them, but I remained where I was and kept still.

I was sorry, because I longed to help the cubs and felt distressed when Elsa looked at me for a long time with a disappointed expression in her eyes and then went out to join her children. Of course she could not understand that my lack of response was due to our wish to preserve the cubs' wild instinct.

The cubs were worried about our relationship for the opposite reason, and became anxious every evening when Elsa, persecuted by tsetse flies, flung herself in front of me, asking me to dispose of these pests.

When I started squashing the flies, and in the process slapping Elsa, the cubs were very upset. Jespah in particular would come close and crouch, ready to spring should his mother be in need of protection.

On one occasion, when Elsa, Jespah, and Little Elsa were drinking in front of the tent, Gopa was too nervous to come to the water bowl. Seeing this, Elsa went to him with great deliberation and cuffed him several times, after which he plucked up enough courage to join the others.

Jespah's character was quite different — he was rather too brave. One afternoon, after they had all fed and their bellies were near bursting point, Elsa started off toward the rock. By then it was nearly dark. Two cubs followed obediently, but Jespah went on gorging. Elsa called twice to him, but he merely listened for a moment and then went on feeding. Finally, his mother came back, and it was in no uncertain manner that she walked up to her son. Jespah realized that he was in for trouble; so, gobbling the meat and with large bits of it hanging out of either side of his mouth, he trotted after her.

At this time I had to go for a few days to Isiolo.

On my way back to camp I was delayed by floods. We had to cross plains where in some places there was a foot of water and in others deep mud. The car often got stuck, and with only Ibrahim and Nuru to help, it sometimes took us hours to dig it out and get it going again.

When we reached the fourth and last river which we had to ford, we found it so high that we dared not attempt the crossing. All we could do was to stop and wait until the water level dropped.

Nuru had only just returned to us; he had been home, ill, for six months. Now he was well again, but he blamed

Elsa for his sickness. This surprised me, as he had always been very devoted to her, but it seemed that the onset of his malady had coincided with the time at which we had engaged him to look after Elsa and her two sisters. Because of this he was convinced that she had cast the "evil eye" on him. It was to dispel this belief that I was now taking him to the camp with me. As we waited in the drizzling rain, I told him about the cubs and he seemed very interested.

During the night the river fell, so we were able to reach camp. Hoping to be able to show Nuru the cubs the next afternoon, we all walked in their direction. Suddenly we heard Elsa talking to them in the bush just ahead of us.

Soon she came bouncing out, and after greeting us made a great fuss over Nuru. Indeed, she was so overwhelmingly happy to see her old friend again after such a long absence that he was very much touched; he began to pat her and discarded all his superstitious fear of her "evil eye." After this reunion he became even more devoted to her than he had been before his illness. She did not, however, show him her cubs on this occasion, and only brought them into camp after dark.

Unlike their mother, the cubs had never had any man-made toys to play with, but they wrestled in the bright lamplight and were never at a loss to find a stick to fight for. At other times they played hide-and-seek and "ambushes." Often they would get locked in a clinch, the victim struggling on his back with all four paws in the air. Elsa usually joined in their games; in spite of her great weight, she sprang and hopped about as though she were herself a cub.

We had provided two water bowls for them, a strong aluminum basin, and an old steel helmet mounted on a piece of wood, which Elsa had used since her youth. This was the more popular of the two with the cubs. They often tipped it over and were alarmed at the clatter it made when it fell. Then, recovering from their fright, they faced the shiny moving object with cocked heads and finally began to prod it cautiously. We took flashlight photographs of these games.

We had more difficulty in taking pictures of them at play during daylight, because they were then less active. Our best chance was in the late afternoon, when they went to a favorite playground near a doum palm which had fallen at the edge of the riverbank, some two hundred yards from the camp. This place overlooked a wide-open space and had thick bush close by, into which the cubs could disappear if any danger threatened. It was also near a salt lick. Besides all this, I often placed a carcass nearby.

George and I used to hide in the bush and take films of the family climbing up and down the fallen trunk and teasing their mother, who was always there to guard them.

As the days passed, I observed that the cubs were getting more and more shy. Now they preferred to sneak through the grass in a wide circle to reach their meat, rather than follow their mother in a straight line, because this involved coming very close to me.

To prevent predators from stealing the meat during the night I started dragging the carcass from the doum palm near to my tent, to which I attached it by a chain. It was often a heavy load, and Elsa used to watch me, apparently content that I had taken on the laborious task of protecting her meat.

Jespah was much less happy when he saw me handling the kill. After several halfhearted attacks he sometimes charged me in a proper fashion, first crouching low and then rushing forward at full speed. Elsa came instantly to my rescue: she not only placed herself between her son and me, but gave him a sound and deliberate cuff. Afterward she sat with me in the tent for a long time, totally ignoring Jespah, who rested outside, looking bewildered. He lay by the helmet bowl, his head against it, occasionally lapping lazily.

Touched as I was by Elsa's reaction, I also understood that Jespah should be disconcerted by his mother's disapproval of his instinctive reaction, and I was most anxious not to arouse his jealousy.

He was still too small to do very much harm, but we recognized that it was essential to establish a friendly truce with the cubs while they were still dependent upon us for food and before they had grown big enough to be dangerous. It was a difficult problem, because while we did not want them to be hostile, neither did we want them to become tame.

Recently Elsa herself seemed to have become aware of our difficulty and to be making her contribution to solving it. While she spanked Jespah if in his attempts to protect her he attacked me, she also dealt firmly with me if she thought I was getting too familiar with her children. For instance, several times when I came close to them while they were at play, she looked at me through half-closed eyes, walked slowly but purposefully up to me, and gripped me around the knees in a friendly but determined manner, which indicated very plainly that her grip would become much firmer if I did not take the hint and retire.

Elsa deals firmly with her "child."

The Personality
of the Cubs

ON April 8 George left for Isiolo. One night Elsa turned up her nose at the meat I offered her. Afterward the boys told me that that goat had been ill; so her instinct had evidently warned her that the meat was infected. The cubs also would not touch it. As a rule they were remarkably greedy, ate enormously, and insisted on being suckled by Elsa as well as eating meat.

Elsa spent that evening resting her head against my shoulder and *mhn-mhn*ing to the cubs, a very sonorous sound although it came through closed lips. Fruitlessly, she tried to make them come to me.

That night after I had gone to bed I heard Elsa's mate calling, but instead of going to him she tried to creep through the thorn fence into my *boma*.[1] I called out, "No,

[1] A word to describe any enclosed habitation.

Elsa, no," and she stopped at once. She then settled her cubs by the wicker gate, and there they spent the night.

The next day she did not appear till after dark, and then only brought two cubs with her. Jespah was missing. Elsa settled down to her meal with Gopa and Little Elsa. I was anxious about Jespah, but in the dark I could not go and look for him, so I tried to induce his mother to do so by imitating his high-pitched "*tciang-tciang*" and at the same time pointing to the bush. After a while she went off. The two cubs did not seem to be worried by her absence and went on eating for at least five minutes before they made up their minds to follow her. A little later Elsa and the two cubs returned, but there was no sign of Jespah.

I then discovered that Elsa had a large thorn stuck deeply into her tail. It must have been very painful, and when I tried to pull it out she became irritable. Luckily, I did eventually manage to extract it; then she licked the wound and afterward my hand, by way of thanking me. By this time Jespah had been missing for one hour.

Suddenly, and without any prompting from me, she and the two cubs walked purposefully off into the bush, and soon I heard Jespah's familiar *tciangs*. Presently he appeared with the others, nibbled at some meat, and came to lie within five feet of me. I was thankful to see him safely back, as the hour he had chosen to go off on his own was the most dangerous as far as predators are concerned, and he was still much too young to tackle even a hyena, let alone a lion.

To provide him with something harmless to do, I got an old inner tube and wiggled it near him. He attacked it at once, and soon his brother and sister joined in the new game. They fought and pulled until there was nothing left but shreds of rubber.

That night it rained. In the morning I was much surprised to see not only Elsa's pugmarks but those of a cub inside George's empty tent. It was the first time that one of them had entered the self-imposed forbidden area.

On the following night Elsa, observing that the boys had forgotten to place thorn branches in front of the entrance to my enclosure, pushed the wicker gate aside, entered the tent, and promptly lay down on my bed. Wrapped up in the torn mosquito netting, she looked so content that I saw myself having to spend the night sitting in the open.

Jespah followed his mother into the tent and stood on his hind legs examining the bed, but fortunately decided against trying it out. The other cubs stayed outside.

We spent most of the evening trying to lure Elsa out of my tent. For some time our hopes of success were pretty dim. Then I began to make *tcianging* noises around the camp and to flash my torch, pretending that the cubs were lost and that I was looking for them. This soon caused both Elsa and Jespah to rush out. She came through the door; how he got out I do not know.

I now had my tent to myself, but was unable to sleep because Elsa noisily attacked my truck. However, she stopped when I shouted, "No, Elsa, no," to her. I could not understand why she went for the goats' truck, for if she were hungry there was still some meat down by the river.

The cubs were about sixteen weeks old, and by now the family should have been guarding its kill. Had Elsa become so lazy that she expected us not only to provide her with food but also to relieve her of the task of protecting it? Were we ruining her wild instincts and should we leave her?

The moment did not seem a propitious one for deserting her, because we had recently found the footprints of two strange Africans very near the camp. The drought was again with us, and probably they intended to bring their stock into the game reserves to graze, though this was illegal. Under the circumstances, I felt I must go on providing the family with food; if not, Elsa would surely kill some trespassing goat. I comforted myself with the thought that very soon the seasonal rains would come, the tribesmen would go away, and by the next dry season Elsa would have the cubs well on the run to hunt with her.

Meanwhile I was immensely interested in observing their development. Already they stretched their tendons; they stood on their hind legs and dug their claws into the rough bark of certain trees, preferably acacias. In so doing, they exposed the pink bases of their claws. When they had finished this exercise, the bark showed deep gashes.

The cubs were very easily distinguishable. Jespah was much the lightest in color. His body was perfectly proportioned, and he had a very pointed nose and eyes so acutely slanted that they gave a slightly Mongolian cast to his sensitive face. His character was not only the most nonchalant, daring, and inquisitive, but also the most affectionate. When he was not cuddling up against his mother and clasping her with his paws, he demonstrated his affection to his brother and sister.

When Elsa ate I often saw him pretending to eat too, but he was in fact only rubbing himself against her. He followed his mother everywhere like a shadow.

His timid brother Gopa was also most attractive; he had very dark markings on his forehead, but his eyes, instead of being bright and open like Jespah's, were rather clouded and squinted a little. He was bigger and more heavily built than his brother. Though he was by no means stupid, he took a long time to make up his mind and, unlike Jespah, was not venturesome.

Little Elsa fitted her name, for she was a replica of her mother at the same age. She had the same expression, the same markings, the same slender build. Her behavior, too, was so strikingly like Elsa's that we could only hope she would develop the same lovable character. She knew of course that for the moment she was at a disadvantage compared to her two stronger brothers, but she used cunning to restore the balance.

Though all the cubs were well disciplined and obeyed Elsa instantly on all important occasions, when playing they showed no fear of her, and were only occasionally intimidated by the cuffs she gave them when they became too cheeky.

By the time the cubs were eighteen weeks old Elsa seemed to have become resigned to the fact that their relationship with us would never be the same as ours with her.

Indeed, they were growing more shy every day and preferred to eat outside the area lit by our lamp, except for Jespah, who, as he followed his mother everywhere, often came with her into the "danger zone." Elsa now often placed herself between us and the cubs in a defensive position.

As they were in excellent condition, we thought that we should risk leaving them to hunt with Elsa, for a few days, anyway. Their father had been about lately, and as the family had only come into camp for short feeding visits, we assumed that they were spending most of their time with him.

While the boys were breaking camp I went to the studio, and sitting on the ground, with my back against a tree, started reading a huge bundle of letters from readers of *Born Free*. They had come up with the Land Rover, which had arrived to transport our belongings. I was worrying about how I should find time to answer them all, as I wanted to, when suddenly I was squashed by Elsa. As I struggled to free myself from beneath her three hundred pounds, the letters were scattered all around the place; and when I had got onto my feet again and began to collect them, Elsa bounced onto me every time I bent down to pick one up, and we rolled together on the ground. The cubs thought this splendid fun and dashed around after the fluttering paper. I thought that Elsa's admirers would have enjoyed seeing how much their letters were appreciated. In the end, I am glad to say that I recovered every one of them; I sent for Elsa's dinner and this diverted her attention.

Jespah (left), Gopa (right), Little Elsa (behind).

Elsa Meets Her
British Publisher

AFTER a five-day absence we returned on April 28 to camp; ten minutes later Elsa arrived alone. She was in excellent condition and delighted to see us, but made away with the carcass we had brought for her before we had time to tie it up for the night.

She did not reappear for twenty-four hours. Then she came alone, ate enormously, and by the morning was gone.

The absence of the cubs worried us, but the next afternoon we found the whole family playing in a dry riverbed. They followed us back to the camp. Soon afterward a thunderstorm broke out. Elsa at once joined us in our tent, but the cubs sat outside, at intervals shaking the water off their coats. No one looks his best when drenched and cold, but the cubs certainly looked most endearing, if rather pathetic: their ears and paws seemed twice their normal size against their soaking bodies. As soon as the worst of the downpour was over, Elsa joined them and they had an energetic game together, perhaps to warm themselves.

After this they settled down to their dinner and tore at the meat so fiercely that beneath their coats, which now were dry and fluffy, we could see the play of their well-developed muscles. At the end of their meal, for the first time we saw them bury the uneaten part of the kill. They scratched sand over the little pile most carefully until nothing of it could be seen. Perhaps their mother had taught them to do this during the five days in which they had lived totally wild. After everything had been neatly cleaned up, the cubs settled around Elsa and she suckled them for a long time.

We wanted to feed Elsa up before another absence, so early one morning we called to her from the foot of the Big Rock. She came down with Jespah at her heels; the other two kept at a little distance. For a time they followed us along the car track, the cubs gamboling and wrestling, and Elsa often pausing to wait for them.

Full of *joie de vivre*[1] the cubs bustled along, knocking each other over, until Elsa turned into the bush, probably intending to take a short cut to the camp. Little Elsa and Gopa chased after her, but Jespah stayed on the track. It seemed that he felt in charge of his pride, and we were certainly not included. He was making sure that we were not following his family. He paid no attention to his mother's call and advanced toward us in a most determined fashion, sometimes crouching low and then making a short rush forward. When he was quite close he stopped,

[1] Joy of living.

looked at us, and rolled his head from side to side. He appeared embarrassed and as though he did not know what he should do next. Meanwhile Elsa returned to fetch her disobedient son, who, having stepped nimbly aside to avoid a vigorous cuff, trotted after his brother and sister.

We spent a happy day in the studio, where the family gorged on a carcass. When they could eat no more, the cubs rolled on their backs and with paws in the air dozed off; I leaned against Elsa's stern, and Jespah rested under her chin.

As soon as the cubs recovered from their siesta, they explored the low branches which overhang the rapids halfway across the river. They seemed to have no fear of heights or of the rushing water below and turned with the greatest ease on even the thinnest boughs.

The next afternoon I saw Elsa through my field glasses. She was on the ridge outlined against the sky, watching intently a little gap between some rocks. Then suddenly her attention became fixed in the direction of the track; probably she heard the sound of George's car returning from patrol.

Soon it appeared, stopped, and I got into it and began talking to George. In the back I observed some guinea fowl which he had shot, and looked forward to a pleasant change from the canned food on which we were living.

But with a rush Elsa had leaped between us and was among the birds. Feathers began to fly in all directions as she jumped about making frantic efforts to pluck the birds. It looked as though nothing would be left of them, so George picked up a guinea fowl and threw it to the cubs. Immediately Elsa rushed after it and we took the opportunity to start up the engine and move off. Seeing this, Elsa bounded onto the roof of the Land Rover and insisted on being driven home. We hoped that after we had gone a few hundred yards her motherly instinct would make her return to the cubs, but she felt far from motherly, and we had to bang on the inside of the canvas roof until we made her quite uncomfortable, before she decided to jump off and rejoin her bewildered family.

Later they all came to camp and had great fun with the guinea fowl. We were amused to observe how very cunning Little Elsa had become. She allowed her brothers to pull out the prickly quills of the feathers and then, when the bird had been nicely plucked, took the first opportunity of grabbing it.

After this she defended it with snarls, growls, and scratchings, her ears flattened, and with such a forbidding expression that the "boys" thought it wiser to go off and pluck another bird.

Sometimes the fights between the cubs over food were quite rough, but they never sulked afterward or showed any resentment. We were surprised that they preferred guinea fowl to goat meat. When she was a cub, Elsa had regarded a dead guinea fowl merely as a toy and seldom considered eating it.

The family spent that night close to the camp, and in the morning we thought we knew why, for father's pugmarks were all around the place, and we assumed that he had intended to share their meal. Elsa had obviously not been agreeable to this plan, for she had dragged a carcass into a thicket between our tents and the river, where it was unlikely that he would care to come.

Elsa remained with her cubs in this stronghold for the next twenty-four hours, and only left it when she heard George returning from patrol in his Land Rover. He had brought some more guinea fowl, and the fun and feast of the night before were repeated.

On our return to Isiolo, we were thrilled to hear that a call from London had come through three times in the last few days and was now booked for the next morning.

To speak to someone in England, four thousand miles away, is very exciting when one is in a remote outpost. The voice we heard was that of Billy Collins, our London publisher, accepting our invitation to come out and meet Elsa. For his arrival we fixed a day during the following week; this would make it possible for him to be with us on our next visit to Elsa.

Next morning we arrived in camp. George fired a shot to notify Elsa of the fact, and soon we heard her *hnk-hnk*, but she did not turn up. As her voice came from the direction of the studio, I went to it and saw her and the cubs by the river, drinking. She glanced at me and went on lapping, as though she were not in the least surprised to see me after eight days' absence.

But later she came up and licked me, and Jespah settled himself about a foot away; then she sprang onto the table and lay stretched at full length on it. Jespah stood on his hind legs and rubbed noses with her. Around midnight George woke up to find Elsa sitting on his bed and licking him, while the cubs sat outside the tent watching her.

In the morning I set off with Ibrahim, Makedde, and the cook to meet Billy Collins. When we arrived in the little Somali village where we expected the airplane to land,

I told the Africans to keep the airstrip free of livestock, as a plane might arrive at any moment.

About teatime we heard the vibrations of an engine, but it was a long time before the circling aircraft landed. Then the airstrip was suddenly covered by the entire village population, chattering excitedly. The colorful turbaned Mohammedans, clad in loose-falling garments, watched Billy Collins and the pilot clamber out from the small cabin. As we had a long and rough trip ahead of us, we stopped only for a quick tea at the government guest-house and soon set off.

After two or more hours of brushing and winding our car through thick bush, we arrived at camp; and a few moments later Elsa came rushing along, followed by her cubs. She welcomed us in her usual friendly manner, and after a few cautious sniffs also rubbed her head against Billy, while the cubs watched from a short distance. Then she took the meat and dragged it out of the lamplight into the dark near my tent, where she settled with her children for their meal. While this went on we had our supper. We had made a special thorn enclosure next to George's tent for Billy's tent and, after introducing him to his home, barricaded his wicker gate from outside with thorns and left him to a well-deserved night's sleep.

Elsa remained outside my tent enclosure, and I heard her talking softly to her cubs until I fell asleep.

At dawn I was wakened by noises from Billy's tent and recognized his voice and George's: evidently they were trying to persuade Elsa to leave Billy's bed. As soon as it got light she had squeezed herself through the densely woven wicker gate and hopped onto Billy's bed, caressing him affectionately through the torn mosquito net and holding him prisoner under her heavy body. Billy kept admirably calm, considering it was his first experience of waking up with a fully grown lioness resting on him. Even when Elsa nibbled him slightly in his arm, her way of showing her affection, he did nothing but talk quietly to her.

Soon she lost interest and followed George out of the enclosure, where she romped around the tents with her cubs.

Before dawn the next day I was again waked up by noises coming from Billy's tent, into which Elsa had once more found her way to say good morning. After some coaxing from George, who had come to his rescue, she left. George then reinforced the thorns outside the wicker gate. But Elsa was not going to be defeated by a few thorns, and so after a short time Billy found himself again being embraced by her and squashed under her weight. While he struggled to free himself from the entangling mosquito net, George came to his rescue once more; but by the time he got inside, Elsa had managed to clasp her paws around Billy's neck and held his cheekbones between her teeth. We had often watched her doing this to her cubs — it was a sign of affection — but the effect on Billy must have been very different.

I was very much alarmed at Elsa's unusual behavior. She had never done anything like this to a visitor, and I could only interpret it as a sign of affection. But whatever her motive may have been, I was very upset and remained with Billy in his tent until Elsa, I hoped, had taken her cubs away for the day.

Jespah comes to rub noses with Elsa.

In spite of my precaution she forced herself a third time through the wicker gate before either George, who was outside, or I, who was inside, could stop her. Billy was standing up by this time and, being tall and strong, braced himself against Elsa's weight when she stood on her hind legs, resting her front paws on his shoulders, and nibbled at his ear. As soon as she released him I gave her such a beating that she sulkily left the tent and in a rather embarrassed way spent her affection now on Jespah, rolling with him in the grass, biting and clasping him exactly as she had done to Billy. Finally, the whole family gamboled off toward the rocks.

We certainly did not want to risk a repetition of her demonstrations toward our friend, so we decided to break his visit short and leave camp immediately after breakfast.

"Leave us alone!"

The Camp Is Burned

AT the beginning of June we returned to camp. As we reached a place about six miles short of it, we saw that every tree and bush was loaded with birds of prey. Then suddenly we found ourselves surrounded by elephants. They had closed in on us from every direction — some thirty or forty head. They had a large number of very young calves with them, whose worried mothers came close to the car with raised trunks and fanning ears, shaking their heads angrily at us. It was a tricky situation. George at once jumped onto the roof of the Land Rover and stood there, rifle in hand. We waited for what seemed an endless time, then some of the elephants started to cross the car track about twenty yards from us.

It was a magnificent sight. The giants moved in single file, jerking their massive heads disapprovingly in our direction. To protect their young, they kept them closely wedged between their bulky bodies.

After making infuriated protests, most of the herd moved away, leaving small groups still undecided in the bush. We waited for them to follow, and eventually all but two went off.

George wanted to see the kill which had attracted the birds, and since the light was failing he decided to walk, with Makedde, between the two remaining groups of elephants. He found a freshly killed waterbuck, and lion spoor around it. Very little had been eaten, so plainly the lion had been interrupted by the arrival of the elephants.

We wondered whether Elsa had killed the waterbuck, but it was far from her usual hunting ground. Besides, for her to tackle a beast with such formidable horns and heavier than herself (the buck must have weighed about four hundred pounds), while protecting her cubs, would have been very dangerous. We felt sure she would not have done such a thing unless she were very hungry indeed.

As soon as we got to camp we fired a signal to Elsa, but that night she failed to appear.

Next morning we started off early to investigate the kill. Very little was left of it, and the ground had been so trampled by elephants that we could not distinguish any spoor other than theirs. After a search which lasted for several hours we did find one pugmark of a lion cub. It could have been Jespah's, but we did not believe he would have walked so far.

After our return to camp we were greatly relieved to see Elsa and her cubs on the Big Rock. As soon as she spotted us she rushed down and ended by throwing the whole of her weight against George, who was squashed by her affection. Then she bowled me over, while the puzzled cubs craned their heads above the high grass to see what was going on.

We provided a meal for them, and they competed over it with growls, snarls, and spankings. Little Elsa had the best of it and eventually went off with her loot, leaving her brothers still so hungry that we felt obliged to produce another carcass for them.

That evening Elsa took up her usual position on the roof of the Land Rover, but the cubs, instead of romping about, flung themselves on the ground and never stirred. We were surprised, as it was the hour at which they were usually most energetic. Then, during the night, I heard Elsa talking to them in a low moan and also heard suckling noises. They must indeed have been hungry to need suckling after consuming two goats in twenty-four hours.

In the morning they had gone. We followed their spoor, and it led straight to the waterbuck. So it must have been Elsa who had tackled this formidable beast. It was hard luck that the arrival of the elephants had prevented her and the cubs from having a good meal out of their kill.

Now we understood why they had all been both so hungry and so exhausted when they came into camp.

We collected the fine horns of the waterbuck and hung them in the studio, a proud record of the cubs' first big hunt with their mother.

One evening, when Elsa and her cubs were walking back with us, she and Jespah got in front of us while Gopa and Little Elsa stayed behind. This worried Jespah very much; he rushed to and fro trying to marshal his pride, until his mother stood still, between us and him, and allowed us to pass her, thus reuniting the family. Afterward she rubbed our knees affectionately, as though to thank us for having taken the hint.

Since the cubs' birth we had never used the radio when they were in camp, so as not to frighten them. But next morning George turned on the morning news. Elsa appeared at once, looked at the instrument, roared at it full strength, and went back to the cubs. After a while George tuned in again, whereupon Elsa rushed back and repeated her roars until he switched it off.

I patted her and spoke reassuringly to her in a low voice, but she was not satisfied till she had made a thorough search inside the tent. Then she went to her family.

This reaction of hers was unexpected. Before her release, when she was living with us, we had listened daily to the radio, and though when we first tuned in she had always been startled, as soon as she realized where the sounds came from she had paid no attention to them.

On June 20 the cubs were six months old; to celebrate their first half year George shot a guinea fowl. Little Elsa, of course, took possession of it and disappeared into the bush. Her indignant brothers went after her but returned defeated, and, tumbling down a sandy bank, landed on their mother. She was lying on her back, her four paws straight up in the air. She caught the cubs and held their heads in her mouth. They struggled to free themselves and then pinched their mother's tail. After a splendid game together, Elsa got up and walked up to me in a dignified manner and embraced me gently, as though to show that I was not to be left out in the cold. Jespah looked bewildered. What could he make of this? Here was his mother making such a fuss over me, I couldn't be bad; but all the same I was so different from them. Whenever I turned my back on him, he stalked me, but each time I turned and faced him he stopped and rolled his head from side to side, as though he did not know what to do next. Then he seemed to find the solution: he would go off. He walked straight into the river, evidently intending to cross to the other bank. Elsa rushed after him. I shouted, "No, no," but without effect, and the rest of the family quickly followed them. Young as he was, Jespah had now taken on the leadership of the pride and was accepted by the family.

When they returned, Elsa dozed off with her head on my lap. This was too much for Jespah. He crept up and began to scratch my shins with his sharp claws. I could not move my legs because of the weight of Elsa's head resting on them, so in an effort to stop him I stretched my hand slowly toward him. In a flash he bit it and made a wound at the base of my forefinger. It was lucky that I always carry sulfanilamide powder with me, so I was able to disinfect it at once. All this happened within a few inches of Elsa's face, but she diplomatically ignored the incident and closed her eyes sleepily.

I stayed on beside the river, watching the last glow of the sinking sun gild the tips of the doum palms; then all color vanished and darkness fell.

After this we all returned to camp and Jespah seemed so friendly that I began to wonder whether he had bitten me in play. Certainly between himself and his mother, biting was proof of affection.

By now we were, however, beginning to worry about

his relationship to us. We had done our best to respect the cubs' natural instincts and not to do anything to prevent them from being wild lions, but inevitably this had resulted in our having no control over them. Little Elsa and her timid brother were as shy as ever and never provoked a situation which required chastisement. But Jespah had a very different character. I could not push his sharp, scratching claws back by saying "No", as I used to do when Elsa was a cub, and so teaching her to retract her claws when she was playing with us.

On the other hand, I did not want to use a stick. Elsa might resent it if I did, and indeed she might cease to trust me. Our only hope seemed to lie in establishing a friendly relationship with Jespah.

I had two weeks by myself at Isiolo, after which I planned to meet George in the first week of July at the camp. He would then be returning from routine patrol, and on his way to Isiolo to get ready for a safari to the north.

As I approached the camp I was worried because I did not see George. I drove on, filled with foreboding, which increased as I drew nearer, for the air was full of smoke.

When we arrived I could hardly believe my eyes. The thorn bushes were in ashes, and smoldering tree trunks added to the grilling heat. In the charred and blackened scene the green canvas of the tents stood out in sharp contrast. I was much relieved when I found George inside one of them eating his lunch.

He had plenty to tell me. When he had arrived, two days earlier, he had found the camp burning and seen the footprints of twelve poachers. Not only had they set fire to the trees and the thorn enclosure, but they had also destroyed everything they could find. They had even uprooted the little vegetable garden that Ibrahim had planted.

George had been very worried about Elsa and had fired several thunder flashes between seven and ten P.M. without getting any response. Then at eleven she and the cubs had suddenly appeared, all ravenously hungry. Within two hours they had eaten an entire goat. Elsa had been most affectionate, and had several times come to lie on George's bed during the night; he noticed that she had several wounds. She left at dawn.

Then he went off to try to discover where she had come from on the previous evening. Her spoor, which led down from the river, was mixed up with the footprints of the poachers. He wondered whether they had been hunting Elsa and the cubs.

After lunch he sent three Game Scouts to search for the camp burners. They returned with six of the culprits. George kept them busy rebuilding the camp, which was no agreeable task, considering the amount of thorny bush which they were obliged to cut for our enclosures.

Elsa and her cubs had spent the night in camp and left soon after daybreak. Half an hour later George heard roars coming from the direction of the Big Rock, which was the way they had gone, so he assumed it must be Elsa. He was therefore much astonished to hear her voice coming from across the river soon afterward.

Then she appeared, wet and without the cubs, and seemed very agitated. In a few minutes, she left hurriedly, rushing toward the Big Rock, calling loudly. George felt sure that she must recently have had an encounter with an enemy, for her wounds were not made by a quarry. He thought the roars he had at first taken for Elsa's were probably those of some fierce lion who had attacked her — that while the two were fighting, the cubs had scattered, and that after the battle Elsa had escaped across the river. Now he followed Elsa in search of her family.

Together they climbed up the Big Rock. When they got to its top, Elsa called in a very worried tone of voice. Of the cubs there was no sign. George and Elsa searched back and forth between the rocks and the camp. Suddenly she became much interested in a patch of dense bush, which she sniffed attentively and then called toward. George investigated it, but he saw no sign of the cubs inside the thicket.

Later he and Elsa crept along the ridge, looking into all possible hide-outs. They found the spoor of a large lion and of a lioness, and Elsa seemed most upset.

At the end of the rock, near the place where the cubs had been born, Elsa sniffed very persistently into a cleft. Suddenly George saw one cub peeping over the top of the rock above them, and soon another appeared; they were Little Elsa and Gopa. Jespah was missing.

When they saw their mother they rushed down and rubbed noses with her, and finally went off with her toward the kitchen *lugga*.

All this had taken place just before I had arrived, and as soon as he had finished his lunch George intended to look for Jespah. Naturally I went with him.

Elsa and the two cubs had settled on the top of the ridge; George went off to search for Jespah by the Zom

Rocks. I noticed that Elsa was pulling a grimace and scenting in the direction of the thicket, but when I called up to her she did not budge. The ground was covered with fresh lion spoor, so I understood why she was frightened. However, after George returned she and the two cubs joined us below the rock.

Now she trotted ahead of us toward the interesting thicket. Just after she had passed it I suddenly saw that not two but three cubs were scampering behind Elsa, in the most casual manner. Jespah's reappearance after a day's absence seemed to be taken by the family as the most natural thing in the world. We, however, were greatly relieved, and followed them to the river, where they stopped for a long drink while we went ahead to prepare a carcass for them in camp.

When finally we were able to sit down and enjoy our dinner we discussed Elsa's curious behavior. Why had she not persevered in the search for Jespah? Had she known all the time that he was hiding in the thicket? Why had he not answered his mother's call and ours? Had the strange lions still been near the rocks? This would explain Elsa's fears and Jespah's, but it was unlikely, since the other two cubs had chosen to take refuge there.

After dinner George had to start back for Isiolo to prepare for his three weeks' safari.

During these days I made some attempts to shoot crocodiles, but without much success. When it was getting dark, we were all sitting near the river. Suddenly Elsa and the cubs looked at the water, stiffened, and pulled grimaces, and three or four yards away I saw a croc. I knew he must be a big fellow, for his head was about a foot long.

I fetched my rifle and killed him; the cubs were less than three feet from me, but the shot did not upset them. Elsa afterward came and rubbed her head against my knee, as though to thank me.

It was about this time that Jespah became more friendly. Now he sometimes licked me, and once even stood on his hind legs to embrace me. Elsa took great care not to show too much affection to me in the presence of the cubs, but when we were alone she was as devoted as usual. Her trust in me was as complete as ever, and she even allowed me to take her meat from her claws and move it to a more suitable spot when I thought this necessary. She also permitted me to handle the cubs' meat. For instance, in the evening, when I wanted to remove a

Cub drinks warily from the bowl.

partly eaten carcass from the riverbank so that the crocs should not finish it off, she never interfered, even though the cubs were hanging on to it and defending it.

At dusk the cubs were always full of energy, and played tricks on their mother that made it hard for her to retain her dignity. Jespah, for instance, discovered that when he stood on his hind legs and clasped her tail she could not easily free herself. In this fashion they would walk around in circles, Jespah behaving like a clown, until Elsa had had enough of it and sat down on top of him. He seemed to be delighted by her way of putting an end to the game, and would lick and hug his mother until she escaped into our tent.

But it was not long before the tent ceased to provide her with an asylum, for Jespah followed her into it, giving a quick look around and then sweeping everything he could reach to the ground. During the night I often heard him busily engaged in sorting through the food boxes and the beer crate; the clattering bottles provided him with endless entertainment. One morning the boys found fragments of my precious rubber cushion in the river; but I really could not blame Jespah for this, as I had stupidly forgotten to remove it from my chair the evening before. He became quite at home in the tent, but his brother and sister were less venturesome. They stayed outside watching the fun.

Jespah even visited the boys in the kitchen. He appeared one evening while they were sitting around an open fire, walked around them sniffing, inspected the place thoroughly, and then went off.

Elsa and family rest on the burnt-over ground of the campsite.

Each of the cubs in turn receives Elsa's affection during their siesta.

Elsa's Fight

MAKEDDE had observed vultures circling and, going to the spot about a mile downstream, found the remains of a rhino which had been killed by poisoned arrows the day before.

The poachers had left plenty of footprints and had erected *machans*[1] on trees close to the drinking place. They must have been well informed and known that I was alone with only Makedde to guard the place, for had George been with me they would never have dared to indulge in these activities so close to the camp.

For three days Elsa arrived in camp long after dark, and on the fourth (July 15) brought only two cubs; Jespah was missing. I was very worried, so after waiting for some time, I began repeating his name over and over

[1] Observation platforms in trees, used by hunters.

again, till Elsa decided to go upstream and look for him, taking the two cubs with her.

For over an hour I heard her calling, till the sound gradually receded into the distance.

Then suddenly there were savage lion growls, accompanied by the terrified shrieks of baboons. As it was dark, I could not go to see what was happening, and awaited the outcome feeling miserable, for I was sure that Elsa was being attacked by lions.

She came back after a while, her head and shoulders covered with bleeding scratches and the root of her right ear bitten through. There was a gap in the flesh into which one could stick two fingers. This was much the worst injury she had ever suffered. Little Elsa and Gopa came back with her and sat a short distance away, looking very frightened. I tried to put sulfanilamide into Elsa's wounds, but she was far too irritable to let me come near her; nor was she interested in the meat which I brought her. I placed the carcass halfway between myself and the cubs. They pounced on it, dragged it into the dark, and I soon heard them tearing at it.

I sat a long time with Elsa; she held her head on one side and the blood dripped from her wound. Eventually she rose, called the cubs, and waded across the river.

I could hardly wait till it was light to go and look for Jespah. Next morning, following Elsa's spoor, Makedde, Nuru, and I went to the Cave Rock and were much relieved to find the family reunited. I was happy to know that Jespah was safe and that I could now concentrate on treating his mother. The wound in her ear was still bleeding profusely, and at intervals she shook her head to drain the cavity. Owing to its position, she could not lick the wound but scratched constantly to keep off the flies; none of this was likely to improve the cleanliness of the wounds.

All the cubs seemed very subdued, though Jespah licked his mother affectionately.

We made a detour on our return journey, so as to inspect the previous night's battlefield. We found it on a sandbank in the middle of the river, about half a mile from the camp. There were plenty of lion pugmarks mixed up with baboon spoor, but though we could distinguish the imprints of one male lion, we could not be sure whether he had been alone or not.

I waited anxiously till the late afternoon for Elsa and her family to arrive. I then managed to introduce some M and B tablets into the meat, which she took from my hand. I thought that if I could get fifteen tablets down her daily, there was a good chance that her wound would not go septic. Her ear drooped, suggesting that the muscles had been injured, and she constantly shook her head to get rid of the oozing liquid.

Jespah, who had been the cause of the encounter, was very friendly. He licked me and several times tilted his head, looking straight at me for a long time.

Toward evening Nuru herded the goats toward the truck. This was the first time I had seen the cubs take any interest in them. We had, of course, been careful to avoid any contact between the cubs and living goats, and they had never before reacted to their bleating.

During the night I heard two lions grunting as they cracked the bones of the carcass which was lying in front of George's tent. They spent a long time over their meal, and only went off at dawn when the boys began talking in the kitchen.

Elsa kept away for some days. I thought her absence was explained by the presence of this pair who had remained nearby, and who the following night grunted around the goat truck.

After four days, however, I became very anxious. Elsa's wound must be a handicap to her in hunting, and I was afraid also that the poachers might do her some harm. When on the evening of July 20 I saw vultures circling, my heart sank. We went to investigate, but all we found was more evidence of the poachers. They had constructed hide-outs near to every drinking place, on both sides of the river. We also found ashes of recent fires and charred animal bones.

A week earlier, when Makedde had found poisoned arrowheads in a rhino, I had sent a message to the Warden of the reserve, asking him to send scouts to patrol the area. Now on our return to camp we found that they had arrived, and I was very glad to see them. With our reinforcements we set out next morning to look for Elsa, and arranged that if anyone spotted her they should fire a shot.

Three hours later I heard a report and returned to camp to be told by two of the newcomers that they had seen Elsa and the cubs under a bush on the opposite side of the river, about a mile inland. She was lying in the shade, and the cubs were asleep. She had seen the men approach, but had not moved.

Makedde suggested that we should take some meat to

her, but not enough to satisfy her hunger, and so tempt her to come back to camp. As we approached her lie-up I signaled to the men to stay behind, and called to her.

She emerged, walking slowly, her head bent low to one side. I was surprised and alarmed that she should have settled in such an exposed place where she could easily be seen by poachers. I noticed that her ear had gone septic and was discharging pus; she was obviously in great pain. Besides this, both she and Little Elsa were covered with blowflies. I was able to rid Elsa of hers, but the cub was far too wild to let me help her.

Meanwhile Little Elsa and her brothers fought over the section of carcass we had brought them, and soon there was nothing left for Elsa but polished bones; she looked on resignedly. Jespah thanked me for his meal by licking my hand with his rough tongue. I tried to induce Elsa to come back to camp by calling, *"Maji, chakula, nyama,"* but as she did not move, we went home without her.

As I had taken a lot of photographs, I went to the tent to get another film; then I heard the cubs arrive on the opposite bank and took a short cut down to the river. Suddenly Elsa broke out of a bush and knocked me over. It had obviously made her suspicious that I had returned from a different direction, and she feared for her cubs. She had been nervous all afternoon and was plainly in pain, for whenever the cubs accidentally touched her ear she snarled and cuffed them irritably. Jespah seemed aware of her state and constantly licked her.

By now I had been three weeks alone in camp, and George was overdue. I wished he would return soon, for when his tent was occupied the predators never came near the meat which was tied up close to it. In his absence wild lions prowled around the camp every night; Makedde and Ibrahim could use their rifles if an emergency arose, but I was nervous about their safety.

At last George arrived and was greeted by the roars of a strange lion. Hearing that Elsa had not been seen for several days, he decided to go and look for her, and he was also determined to try to scare off the strange lion and his fierce lioness, who had so often injured Elsa. We knew her and her mate quite well by now, at least by voice, and we were also familiar with their spoor. They ranged along the river for about ten miles. Of course they shared the country with other lions besides Elsa, but this lioness was the only one who kept permanently to the vicinity of the camp. The fierce lioness had lived in this region long before Elsa, but we did not know what Elsa had done to displease her. Perhaps Elsa had interfered with her hunting or her territorial claims, or perhaps the creature was just bad-tempered. Anyway, we were sure now that she had chased Elsa and the cubs over the river and toward the poachers, and that she and her mate had, for several days, taken over the Big Rock.

Next day we searched upstream on the far side of the river. Here, too, there were plenty of lion pugmarks, including those of a lioness with three cubs. They led us five miles from camp to a part of the bush which, so far as we knew, Elsa had never visited. As we approached a baobab tree, we heard the sound of startled animals bolting, and the Toto caught a glimpse of the hindquarters of a lion and of three cubs which could have been Elsa's. They were gone in a flash, and though we called there was no response.

After two more hours' tracking we found that the pride had reassembled in a sandy watercourse. We kept very quiet till we heard the agitated barking of baboons and, simultaneously, the roar of a lion. He was very close to us. His voice was familiar, for we had often heard it at night. He sounded hoarse; the boys used to say that he must have malaria.

George proceeded to stalk the lion, and we came so close that I was nearly deafened by his next roar. Suddenly I caught sight of his hindquarters, only thirty yards away, and the boys actually saw his head and mane.

It is most unusual for a lion to roar at eleven in the morning. This one was evidently calling to a lioness, whom presently we heard replying from the direction of the barking baboons. Hoping it might be Elsa, we by-passed the hoarse lion and had a good look around, but saw nothing.

Finally, tired and thirsty, we sat down and made tea. Here we discussed the two possible explanations of Elsa's disappearance. Rather than stay in camp and risk being mauled by the ill-tempered lioness, she might have decided to share the hazards of the hoarse lion's life, whose spoor might have been the one we found the previous day. That was an optimistic solution to the mystery; a pessimistic alternative was that Elsa had died of her septic ear and the cubs had been adopted by a pair of wild lions.

We spent the next two days covering the boundaries of Elsa's territory, partly on foot and partly by car. We searched on an average of eight hours a day. We learned nothing of Elsa, but a lot about the poachers. We destroyed many of their hide-outs, and in one found a bit of rope which I had used to fasten the wicker gate of my tent enclosure. Indeed, we saw so much evidence of their activities that George decided to send immediately for an antipoaching squad and, as soon as he could, he would establish a permanent Game Scout post on the river.

George left in the last week of July; I continued to search for Elsa. On the evening of the sixteenth day since the disappearance of Elsa and the cubs, I sat in camp in the dark, straining my ears for any hopeful sound. Suddenly there was a swift movement and I was nearly knocked off my chair by Elsa's affectionate greeting. She looked thin but fit. The wound in her ear was healing from the outside, though the center was still septic.

Plainly she was very hungry, for when the boys came toward us with the carcass I had asked for, she rushed at them. I yelled, "No, Elsa, no." She stopped, obediently returned to me, and controlled herself until the meat had been attached to a chain in front of the tent; then she pounced on it and ate voraciously. She seemed to be in a great hurry, gorged herself on half the goat, and then withdrew out of the lamplight and cunningly moved farther away till she finally disappeared in the direction of the studio.

I was immensely relieved to know that she was well, but where were the cubs? Her visit had lasted only half an hour, and I waited long into the night, hoping that she might return with them to finish off the goat. As this did not happen, I eventually carried the remains into my car to save them from being eaten by predators, and went to bed.

At dawn on August 1, I was wakened by the miaowing of the cubs and saw them crawling close to my thorn enclosure. I called to the boys to bring the meat, and joined Elsa, who was watching her youngsters fighting over the meat.

It was soon obvious that what remained of Elsa's last night's supper was not going to satisfy four hungry lions; I ordered Makedde to kill another goat, and managed to keep Elsa quiet while this was going on. Her self-control was astonishing, and only when the men dropped the carcass within ten yards of her did she get up and drag it into the bush near the river.

Little Elsa and Gopa followed her, but Jespah was far too busy crunching bones to pay any heed to what was going on. Only after he had been on his own for some time did he decide to join the family, and straddling what was left of the old kill, took it down to the river.

I sat under a gardenia bush close by, awaiting my chance to introduce some medicine into Elsa's meat to help her septic ear heal. I was relieved but puzzled not to see a single new scratch on her or the cubs, though they must have hunted during all these days when they were absent from camp.

The cubs growled, snarled, and cuffed at each other for the best bits of meat. Living in the bush had certainly made them more wild; now they were constantly on the alert for suspicious sounds.

The two little cubs were shyer than ever and were frightened if I made the least movement, but Jespah came up to me, tilted his head on one side with a questioning look, licked my arm, and plainly wished to remain friends.

The sun was high and it was getting hot. And so, when the cubs had eaten all they could, they had a splendid game in the shallows, ducking, wrestling, splashing, and churning up the water till at last they collapsed in the shade on a rock, where Elsa joined them.

I watched them dozing contentedly with their paws dangling over the boulder — a happier family one could not wish to see.

In order to try to discover what they had been up-to during their long absence, I had asked Makedde to follow the spoor which Elsa had made when she had arrived in camp.

Meanwhile I dressed her wound while she was too sleepy to object to the treatment. When it got dark I went to the tents to hear Makedde's report.

He told me he had traced her to the limit of her "territory," and that there, on some rocky outcrops, he had found not only her pugmarks and those of the cubs, but also the spoor of at least one other lion, if not two.

This probably explained how she and the cubs had been fed. It also accounted for her strange behavior when she was surprised by the Game Scout and by us, for her reactions were typical of a lioness in season.

It may seem odd that this solution had not occurred to us, but as Elsa was still suckling her cubs we had not expected her to be interested in a mate. We had accepted the general belief that wild lionesses only produce cubs every third year, because in the interval they are teaching the young of the last litter to hunt and become independent. Could Elsa have returned more quickly than we expected to breeding condition because of the food we had supplied? Obviously she could not know that we were only staying on to treat her wounds, and help her to get fit and able to teach her cubs hunting.

Many of the cubs' boxing matches took place in the river.

Dangers of the Bush

AT about nine that evening Elsa and the cubs came from the river, settled themselves in front of my tent, and demanded their supper. As the remains of the meat were still by the gardenia bush, I called to Makedde and the Toto and asked them to help me drag in the carcass. I collected a pressure lamp, and we went down the narrow path which we had cut through the dense bush from the camp to the river.

Makedde, armed with a stick and a hurricane lamp, went ahead, the Toto followed close behind, and, carrying my bright light, I brought up the rear. Silently we walked a few yards down the path. Then there was a terrific crash. Out went Makedde's lamp, and a second later mine was smashed as a monstrous black mass hit me and knocked me over.

The next thing I knew, Elsa was licking me. As soon as I could collect myself I sat up and called to the boys. A feeble groan came from the Toto, who was lying close to me holding his head; then he got up shakily, stammering, "Buffalo, buffalo." At this moment we heard Makedde's voice coming from the direction of the kitchen; he was yelling that he was all right. As we pulled ourselves together, the Toto told me that he had seen Makedde suddenly jump to the side of the path and hit out with his stick at a buffalo. The next moment the Toto had been knocked over and then I had been overrun. Luckily the Toto had no worse injury than a bump on his head, caused by falling against a fallen palm trunk. I felt blood running down my arms and thighs and was in some pain, but I wanted to get home before examining my wounds.

This incident certainly belied the popular belief that a lion, however tame, becomes savage at the scent or taste of blood. Elsa, who had obviously come to protect us from the buffalo, seemed to realize that we were hurt and was most gentle and affectionate.

I had no doubt as to the identity of the buffalo, since for several weeks past we had seen the spoor of a bull buffalo going from the studio through the river bush to the sandbank, where a triangular line of impressions marked his drinking place. After quenching his thirst he usually continued upstream, passed below the kitchen, and then settled for the day on a thickly wooded island about half a mile away.

This evening he must have been unusually thirsty and come out very early. Probably Elsa had heard him on the move, and that was why she had brought the cubs into the camp at nine. When he saw us come down to the river with our lamps, the buffalo had evidently been frightened and rushed up the nearest path to safety, only to find us blocking his way.

Elsa came back with us to camp, where we found the cubs waiting for her; how she had prevented them from following her puzzled me.

I was worried about Makedde and went at once to the kitchen to see what condition he was in. There I found him, unhurt and having a splendid time recounting to his awestruck friends his single-handed combat with the buffalo. I am afraid his heroic stature was slightly diminished by the appearance of my bleeding legs, but the main thing was that we were all safe.

I spent a very uncomfortable night, for as well as having painful wounds, all my glands began to swell and it was difficult to find a position in which I could relax, or to breathe without increasing the discomfort of my aching ribs. All the same, I felt rather elated at having acquired a perfect buffalo autograph in the shape of the exact imprint of his hoof.

By the beginning of August, Elsa had become increasingly cooperative, but her son Jespah did not follow her example; every day he became more obstreperous. For instance, Elsa never interfered with our flock of goats, but Jespah now took much too much interest in them.

One evening, when Nuru was herding them toward my truck, Jespah rushed through the kitchen, dodged between the water containers and around the open fire, and arrived at the truck just as the goats were about to enter it.

There was no doubt as to his intentions, so I ran and grabbed a stick, and holding it in front of him shouted, "No, no," in my most commanding voice.

Jespah looked puzzled, sniffed the stick, and began spanking it playfully, which gave Nuru time to lift the goats into the truck. Then Jespah walked back with me to Elsa, who had been watching the game. Often she helped me to control him, either by adding a cuffing to my "noes" or by placing herself between the two of us. But I wondered how long it would be before, even with her support, my commands and my sticks would cease to have any effect. Jespah was so full of life and curiosity and fun; he was a grand little wild lion, and a very fast-growing one too, and it was high time that we left him and his brother and sister to live a natural life. While I was thinking this, he was chasing after the other cubs, and in doing so tipped the water bowl over Elsa, giving her a drenching. He got a clout for his pains, and then she squashed him under her heavy, dripping body. It was a funny sight and we laughed, but this was tactless and offended Elsa, who, after giving us a disapproving look, walked off, followed by her two well-behaved cubs. Later she jumped on the roof of my Land Rover, and I went to make friends again and apologize.

The moon was full, and in the sky the stars sparkled brilliantly, and Elsa, her great eyes nearly black owing to her widely dilated pupils, looked down at me with a serious expression as though saying, "You spoiled my lesson." For a long time I remained with her, stroking her soft silky head.

George now joined me; he had brought an antipoaching team with him. This consists of a sergeant, a driver, and Game Scouts — all Africans. The team is sent wherever its services are most needed, and therefore operates all over the Northern Frontier. The first thing George wanted them to do was to find some man belonging to the tribe on the far side of the river who would be willing to supply information about poachers and other illegal activities which might endanger the lives of wild animals.

The most effective bush telegraph operates throughout the district, based on the services of "informers" who, far from feeling ashamed of their profession, have come to regard themselves almost as auxiliaries of the Game Department. Indeed, informing is an accepted practice, and without informers it would be impossible to control poaching over such a vast area. The informer is well rewarded for accurate information, because he incurs great risks.

Now that the antipoaching team was established there, we had every intention of leaving Elsa and her family to look after themselves. Her wounds were more or less healed, and we wanted the lions to lead a natural life. But when the Scouts returned we found that we had to change our plans. They brought in some prisoners, and an informer told George that the poachers had determined to kill Elsa with poisoned arrows as soon as we left the camp. We realized that as the drought increased, so would the poachers' activities; and however efficient the antipoaching team might be, it would be impossible for them to prevent Elsa, if unfed by us, from hunting farther afield and risking an encounter with the tribesmen.

Obviously, if we stayed on, the cubs' education in wild life would be delayed and they would probably get spoiled, but it was better to face this than risk a tragedy.

One evening the tsetse flies were particularly active, and Elsa and her two sons rolled on their backs inside my tent trying to squash their tormentors. In doing so they knocked down two camp beds which were propped up against the wall. Elsa lay down on one of them and Jespah on the other, while Gopa had to be content with the groundsheet. The sight of two lions lolling in bed, while far from our ideal picture of Elsa's family returned to a wild life, was comic enough. Only Little Elsa stayed outside; she was as wild as ever and nothing would induce her to enter the tent, so she at least appeased my conscience.

About midnight I was waked up by the roaring of several lions. This was followed by the frightening noise of a fight, and after a pause, another fight, and later a third. Finally, I heard the whimpering of a lion who obviously had got hurt in the battle; I could only hope it was not Elsa. Next, there was the sound of an animal crossing the river, and then all was quiet.

At dawn, we got up and went out to track the spoors left by our quarrelsome visitors. We recognized those of the fierce lioness and her mate. Evidently Elsa had challenged them when they neared the camp. For six hours we followed her pugmarks that led across the river to the Border Rocks; they joined up with those of the cubs.

All day we searched fruitlessly, and at sunset fired a shot. After some time we heard Elsa calling from far away, and eventually she appeared, followed by Jespah.

She was limping badly, but seemed to wish to get to us as fast as she could hobble, though she stopped once or twice and looked back to see whether the other two cubs were coming. When they joined us, both she and Jespah showed how pleased they were by rubbing themselves against our legs. I then saw that Elsa had a deep gash in one of her front paws, which was bleeding and obviously causing her a lot of pain. The only way of helping her was to get her home and dress the wound.

The camp was far off, it was getting dark, and judging by the many spoors of buffaloes and rhinos we had seen, it was essential not to get benighted. Everything indicated that we should hurry, but in spite of George's impatient shouts urging us to make haste, we had often to stop and wait for the little ones, whose pace was rather slow. Jespah acted like a sheep dog, running between George and the rearguard, trying to keep us all together.

For once, the tsetse flies were a help. Elsa was covered with them, and so kept up with me in the hope that I would brush them off her back. Jespah, too, was attacked by them, and for the first time pushed his silky body against my legs asking me to deliver him too from this plague. It was all against my principles to touch him, but it was difficult to resist brushing off the flies.

We were all completely exhausted when we got back. Elsa refused to eat, but sat on the Land Rover watching the cubs tearing at the meat and at intervals looking with great concentration into the darkness. It was barely nine when she left the camp with her family, and about midnight we heard a lion calling from the Big Rock.

During the next days Elsa came into camp every afternoon, and I dressed her wounds.

When she was better, she and the cubs came along the river with us on a croc hunt. Then we had another example of the way in which she could apparently order the cubs to stay put and be implicitly obeyed.

She scented a buck and stalked it unsuccessfully; meanwhile the cubs remained as still as though they had been frozen to the ground. There was never a question of their interfering with her hunt, though later they were lively enough splashing in the water and climbing trees. This they achieved by hooking their claws into the bark and pulling themselves up; sometimes they got as high as ten feet above the ground.

Next evening Elsa came in very late and settled near the tents while Jespah, who was in one of his energetic moods, amused himself by upsetting everything within reach. The tables were swished clear of bottles, plates, and cutlery, the rifles were pulled out of their stands and the haversacks full of ammunition carried away, and cardboard containers were first proudly paraded in front of the other cubs and then torn to shreds. In the morning we found the family still in camp — a most unusual occurrence. The boys kept well inside the kitchen fence, waiting for them to go. Then, as they showed no intention of leaving, George walked up to Elsa, whereupon she knocked him down.

After this George released me from my thorn enclosure and I tried my luck. I approached Elsa, calling to her; but as she looked at me through half-closed eyes, I kept on my guard while she came slowly toward me. I was justified, for when she was within ten yards of me she charged at full speed, knocked me down, sat on me, and then proceeded to lick me.

She was extremely friendly, so this, it seemed, was no more than her idea of a morning game. But she knew quite well that the knocking-down trick was not popular with us, and this was the first time since the birth of the cubs that she had indulged in it.

Later she took the cubs to a place below the studio, and in the afternoon we joined them there. Jespah was very much interested in George's rifle and tried his best to snatch it away from him, but soon he realized that it was impossible to do this as long as its owner was on his guard. After this discovery it was amusing to see how he tried to distract George's attention by pretending to chase his brother and sister. When George's suspicions were allayed and he put the rifle down to pick up his camera, Jespah pounced on it and straddled it. A real tug-of-war followed, which Elsa watched attentively.

In the end she came to George's rescue by sitting on her son, thereby forcing him to release his hold on the gun. She continued to sit on the cub for such a long time that I got quite worried about him. When she at last released him, though he looked longingly at the rifle and crouched near it, he was very subdued and left it alone. Nevertheless, for a while Elsa remained suspicious of his good behavior and at intervals placed herself between him and the gun.

Finally, she rolled on her back with her paws in the air and moaned softly. The cubs responded at once and began suckling.

When they dozed off, their round bellies filled to bursting point, Elsa got up, arched her back, gave a long yawn, came over to me, licked me, sat beside me, and rested her paw on my shoulder for some time, then she put her head on my lap and went to sleep. While she and the two small lions slept, Little Elsa kept guard over the family.

That evening we heard the cubs' father calling, and thought it was because he was nearby that Elsa had preferred not to go far afield. For three more days she never left us.

The family rests in camp under the lantern "moon."

"...truly a 'Garden of Eden' atmosphere."

Cubs and Cameras

THERE was truly a "Garden of Eden" atmosphere about life around the precincts of the camp, for the animals who shared this territory with us had got so used to our presence that they often came very close without showing alarm.

The baboons were, of course, our oldest friends. Indeed, we had lived side by side for so long that we no longer paid any attention to each other, unless something unusual happened. At this season the drought was so great that they started digging up the juicy roots of the reeds which grew on the rocks in the river. One old male was the pioneer in this enterprise. He took possession of a boulder on which a lot of reeds grew, pulled these up, and then began to dig energetically for their roots, often kneeling down to bite them off. Then he carefully peeled off their outer skins and stuffed them into his mouth, till his figure resembled a little barrel, and so he got his name: Barrel. Once another male wished to join in the digging, and though much bigger than Barrel, he was plainly afraid of him and waited for him to have his fill before intruding.

Barrel was certainly a despot; he allowed no female to approach the larder, and so, like well-trained Victorian wives, they kept in the background, sitting on the bank in groups of five or six, suckling their babies, scratching each other's fur, and seeking what nourishment they could get from the scanty grasses.

Nearby lived a crocodile, which I knew well and had often unsuccessfully tried to shoot. Now I saw him stretched out to his full length of about eight feet only a short distance from the baboons. I got my rifle and stalked him, but just as I came within range the baboons gave the alarm; and when next day the same thing happened, I began to wonder whether they were acting as lookouts.

Many birds are used by animals as sentinels, and the giraffe often acts as a watchtower for zebra and antelope, but I was surprised that baboons, whose young are such an easy prey to crocodiles, should help one. Of course, fish provide a more easily obtainable meal for the crocs, and perhaps these baboons knew that the croc had eaten his fill.

I never tired of watching these creatures, and every day brought its surprises.

Even now, as I am typing these words, a troop of some fifty baboons are pacing along the bank opposite me. In the middle of them are three bushbuck, a ram, a doe, and their fawn. They seem to have joined the troop for safety, and are not in the least concerned when a baboon brushes past them.

No scene could be more peaceful or further removed from the generally accepted picture of baboons tearing small animals to pieces. I thought that, if it were not threatened by the poachers, wild life here would be ideal, for even the fierce lioness was much less of a danger to Elsa than these men. In any case, she was a natural part of bush life; so are feuds between lions.

It was encouraging to know that Elsa now went out to meet her enemy. We had first noticed this during the third week of August, the night when Elsa and the cubs were eating their supper in front of the tent. Suddenly she growled and went off, and only returned an hour later. During that night I heard two lions approaching camp, and soon afterward a fearful quarrel broke out. Toward dawn I heard Elsa moving the cubs in the direction of the Big Rock. In the afternoon we met her in the bush on her way to camp; her head, especially near her wounded ear, was covered with bleeding bites.

When Elsa joined us in the studio next day she was still very distressed; this had not prevented her from disciplining Jespah with a series of well-aimed clouts when, intrigued by the clatter of my typewriter, he teased me.

Poor Jespah! He still had a lot to learn — not about the wild life that was his, but about the strange world that was ours, and which he showed so great a wish to investigate. One night, for instance, I heard him apparently very busy in George's tent. How busy I only discovered next morning when I noticed that my field glasses were missing. Eventually I found bits of their leather case in the bush below the tent. They bore the imprint of Jespah's milk teeth. Close by lay the glasses, and luckily, by some miracle, the lenses were intact. Yes, there was no doubt that Jespah could be a nuisance, but he was irresistible and one couldn't be cross with him for long.

At eight months he had now lost his baby fluff, but his coat was as soft as a rabbit's. He had begun to imitate his mother and to wish to be treated by us as she was. Sometimes he would come and lie under my hand, evidently expecting to be patted, and though it was against my principles, I occasionally did so. He often wanted to play with me, but though his intentions were entirely friendly I never felt sure that he might not bite or scratch me as he would his own family. He was not like Elsa, who controlled her strength on such occasions, for he was much closer to a wild lion.

We were very interested in observing the different relationships which Elsa's cubs were developing toward us. Jespah, prompted by an insatiable curiosity, had overcome his earlier inhibitions, mixed with us, and was most friendly, but allowed no familiarities.

Little Elsa was truly wild, snarled if we came close, and then sneaked away. Though she was less boisterous than her brothers, she had a quiet and efficient way of getting what she wanted. Once I watched Jespah trying to drag a freshly killed goat into a bush. He pulled and tugged and somersaulted across it, but nothing would move the carcass. Then Gopa came to his aid, and between the two they tried their best, but finally gave up exhausted and sat panting next to it. Now Little Elsa, who had watched their

118

exertions, came along and, pulling hard, straddled the heavy load into a safe place, where she was joined at once by her panting brothers.

Gopa quite often made use of the tent when the tsetse flies were most active, and it was on these occasions that I noticed how jealous he was. For instance, if I sat near Elsa he would look long and scrutinizingly into my eyes with an expression of disapproval; he made it extremely plain that she was his "Mom" and that he would prefer me to leave her alone. One evening I was sitting at the entrance of the tent while he was in the annex at the far end; Elsa lay between us, watching both of us. When Gopa started chewing at the tent canvas, I said as firmly as I could, "No, no"; to my surprise, he snarled at me but stopped chewing. A little later he took up the canvas again, and though my "No" was answered with another snarl, he again stopped.

So far all the cubs responded when we said "No," although we had never enforced our prohibition with a stick or anything else which could frighten them.

The next day, while I was having tea in the studio, Elsa appeared, very wet and unaccompanied by the cubs; but later they came, and we spent a very happy evening around the camp. Jespah behaved as though he owned the place, and even lay down on George's camp bed, which was vacant, as George had gone back to Isiolo.

During the night I heard Elsa calling to the cubs, and walking in circles around the camp and the salt lick. I felt rather worried at hearing no cub noises; I was still more worried when on the following afternoon she arrived alone from across the river. However, my fears were unnecessary, for later they appeared, and the next morning came in early asking for breakfast. After two hours of gorging they left, and in the afternoon the Toto and I followed them and found the family resting on the Whuffing Rock. Elsa soon spotted us, came down, and rubbed herself against me. Jespah came only a short way and then sat halfway down the rock watching us.

After we had returned to camp, George arrived, bringing a truck as well as his car, and, attracted by the noise of the engines, Elsa and the cubs soon turned up. George told me that next morning David Attenborough and Jeff Mulligan were arriving from London and that we were to collect them at the nearest airstrip.

For some time we had been corresponding with David Attenborough about making a film of Elsa and her cubs for the BBC. We had had previous suggestions for filming her, but these we had refused, fearing that the arrival of a large film unit might upset her. The coming of only two people was much less worrying, but even they would need constant protection.

Soon after we had gone to bed we heard a lion roaring upstream and observed that Elsa at once left the camp. Next morning, September 13, George called me early to his tent, and there I saw Elsa in a terrible state — her head, chest, shoulders, and paws covered with deep, bleeding gashes. She appeared to be very weak, and when I knelt beside her to examine her wounds she only looked at me.

We were very much surprised, for we had not heard any growls during the night and were quite unaware that a fight had taken place. When I began to try to dress her wounds, Elsa struggled to her feet and slowly dragged herself toward the river, evidently in great pain. I went at once to mix some M and B tablets with her food, hoping to counter the risk of sepsis in this way, since any external treatment was obviously going to hurt and irritate her. When all was ready I spent twenty minutes looking for her, but could find no trace of her.

Then I had to start off to meet our guests. It was the worst moment to have visitors — let alone film producers — and I feared they might have no chance of doing any work. I greeted them with this depressing news and soon realized that we had been more than lucky in finding two such animal lovers as David and Jeff.

We arrived in camp at lunchtime; George had just returned from a fruitless search for the cubs. While our guests settled in, I went to look for Elsa and found her under a thick bush near the studio. She was breathing very fast and lay quite still as I swished the flies off her wounds. I went back to camp to get water and mix the M and B tablets with her meat.

Poor Elsa! I had never before seen her in so much pain. She made no effort to raise her head, and it was only when I lifted it that she began to drink: then she lapped for a long time. After that she ate the meat, but made it very plain that she did not want company, so I left her.

Since there was nothing more we could do for Elsa, George and I set out to look for the cubs on the other side of the river. We walked, shouting all the names by which we address Elsa, and also calling Jespah. Finally, behind a bush, we caught sight of one cub, but as we approached it bolted. In order not to frighten it further we decided to go home, and hoped that the cubs would make their own way back to their mother. Jespah was the first to do so. About six in the evening he crossed the river and rushed up to Elsa; then we heard another cub miaowing from the far bank. Elsa heard it too and dragged herself to the riverbank and began calling. It was Gopa; when he saw his mother he swam across. I provided some meat which the little lions devoured, but Elsa would not touch it. Instead, she got up on the roof of the Land Rover, which was parked in front of our tents. We had our supper within a few yards of her, but she took no notice of us. Some time after we had gone to bed, George spotted Little Elsa coming into the camp.

During the following day Elsa kept away, and we knew why, for George saw the fierce lioness on the Big Rock. That night we heard the lioness roaring. We were very worried about Elsa, so as soon as it was light we went to try and find her.

We picked up Elsa's spoor half a mile beyond the Border Rock. I began calling, and presently she came out from behind some rocks. She reconnoitered the neighborhood to see whether all was safe, and then the cubs appeared. They were terribly thirsty. I could not pour out the water we carried quickly enough, and I had some difficulty in avoiding getting scratched and in preventing the plastic water bowl from being torn out of my hands.

Elsa's wounds had improved, but still needed dressing. It took a lot of coaxing to get the family to follow us, and we made our way slowly back to camp. Nuru stayed with me as gun bearer, but when I thought we were nearly home I told him to go on.

I felt a little uneasy after he had left, and then became really worried, for I found that I had miscalculated the distance and had lost myself in the bush. By then it was midday and very hot, and the lions stopped under every bush to pant in the shade. I knew that the best thing to do was to find the nearest *lugga* and follow it, for it must lead to the river, from which I would be able to get my bearings. Fairly soon I came upon a narrow *lugga* and walked along between its steep banks; Elsa followed me, and the cubs scampered along some way behind her.

I had turned a bend when I suddenly found myself standing face to face with a rhino. There was no question of "jumping nimbly aside and allowing the charging beast to pass," as one is supposed to do in such encounters, so I turned and ran back along my tracks just as fast as I could with the snorting creature puffing behind me. At last I saw a little gap in the bank, and before I knew I had done it, I was up it and running into the bush. At this moment the rhino must have seen Elsa, for it swerved abruptly, turned around, and crashed up the opposite side. Elsa stood very still, watching the pair of us. I was extremely glad that she had not followed her usual habit of chasing any rhino she saw.

A few moments later I was greatly relieved to see Nuru coming toward me. I was going to thank him for running to my rescue, but before I had time to speak he told me that he had met a rhino and been chased by it, and that this was what had brought him to where I was. We had a good laugh over our frights and then, keeping close together, we went back to camp.

After a belated lunch we went down to the studio, where camp beds had been put out for a siesta. The beds were set out in a row; mine was on the outside, David's in the middle, and George's beyond his. Jeff was some way off, loading the cameras. Soon I fell asleep, but woke up very suddenly to find a wet Elsa sitting on top of me, licking me affectionately, and keeping me a prisoner under her immense weight. David quickly got the cameras working as Elsa made a bound onto George and greeted him affectionately. Then she walked in a most dignified manner up to the tents and settled herself inside one of them. She completely ignored our guests, and behaved the same way later in the evening. She had been inside a tent with Jespah. Coming out, she passed within six inches of Jeff's feet, but did not take the slightest notice of him.

Next morning we followed Elsa's spoor and found her halfway up the Whuffing Rock, sleeping. As we did not wish to disturb her, we went home and came back again after tea with a sufficient number of cameras to take films from every angle.

We were very lucky, for Elsa and the cubs could not have been more obliging; they posed beautifully on the saddle of the rock. Finally Elsa came down, and this time she greeted all of us, including David and Jeff, by rubbing her head gently against our knees. She stayed with us until it got dark and we went back to camp.

Although Elsa had not seemed upset by being filmed, I wondered whether she would come for her evening meal. I need not have worried; just as I was going to explain to our guests that she might very well not turn up, I was nearly knocked over by her stormy greeting.

I mixed a dish of her favorite meat with some cod-liver oil and was taking it to her when Jespah ambushed me and licked the dish.

While this was happening, Jeff was testing the sound recorder and happened to run through some recordings of the fierce lioness roaring. Jespah cocked his ears and tilted his head sideways as he listened attentively to the hated voice. Then he left his tidbits and rushed to warn his mother of the danger.

I was most interested to observe that Jespah reacted just as Elsa used to when she was a cub; he knew at once whether someone liked him, felt a bit nervous of him, or was really frightened — and treated him accordingly. David, I am sorry to say, he singled out for stalking and ambushing, and most of David's time was spent trying to dodge Jespah.

On their last evening our guests said good-bye to Elsa while she was sitting on the Land Rover — they shook her paw, and I felt that she had become more to them than a mere film attraction.

The cubs share an evening drink at the pool.

Skirmish
with Poachers

DURING the night of September 21 we heard a lion roaring, and the next day George found the spoor of a male lion near the camp. Later the Toto and I went in search of Elsa and found her on the Whuffing Rock, but though I called to her and climbed up to her, she paid no attention. I went home wondering whether Elsa's mate might be nearby, and if this was the explanation of her behavior. She did not come into camp that night, but next afternoon we saw the family playing in the river. While the cubs splashed about and fought over floating sticks, Elsa placed herself near to the Toto in a position from which she could keep an eye on all of us.

As we walked home, Jespah became very much interested in the Toto's rifle and persistently stalked and ambushed him. Elsa came to the rescue several times and sat on her son long enough to allow the Toto to get well ahead unmolested.

That evening the tsetse flies were particularly annoying, and Elsa flung herself on the ground inside my tent, miaowing for help in getting rid of them. I came in to perform my task, but Jespah and Gopa had already rushed up to their mother and were rolling around squashing the flies. When I approached Elsa they snarled at me; and when I began to deal with the tsetse she began licking the cubs, no doubt to quiet their jealousy.

It was about this time that I began to notice how very jealous Gopa was growing, not only of me but also of his brother. When Jespah played with their mother he would push his way between the two of them, and when Elsa came close to me he crouched and snarled until she went over to him.

After George went away I slept in the Land Rover, close to which the carcass was chained at night; by doing so I hoped to preserve it from chance predators. This arrangement did not make for undisturbed sleep, but it gave me a wonderful opportunity of seeing the nocturnal creatures of the bush.

I particularly liked a civet cat, an exceptionally dark-colored and fierce one which used to take possession of the kill, to the exasperation of the circling jackals. It had only to raise its head for them to bolt away as fast as they could. To be able to watch this interesting animal I used to allow it to have a good meal, but I was much less generous to the hyenas and the jackals.

One night I was waked up by the sound of breaking trees and the trumpeting of elephants. They were down by the river, between the studio and the tents, but gradually moved nearer. This worried me, for I could not think what I should do if they came up to the tents. Elsa sat with her cubs by my "sleeper," facing the noise and perhaps harboring similar misgivings. We all listened intently. Suddenly I saw a huge shape moving along the top of the bank; it stopped and stood still for what seemed an endless time, then it vanished into the darkness.

Soon afterward my torchlight was reflected in a pair of green eyes which gradually came closer. Assuming it to be a prowling predator, I got out of the car, intending to cover the carcass with thorns, but before I had dragged one big branch into position, Elsa bounced on me. I climbed back into my bedroom; then, when she and the cubs seemed to have finished their meal and gone away, I came out again, for I was determined not to give a free meal to the jackals. Once more Elsa jumped on me and defended her kill. We spent the rest of the night watching each other. She won the game, but probably at the cost of eating a lot more than she wanted.

By October both Billy Collins and I felt that it would be useful to meet and discuss plans for the sequel to *Born Free*. I went to Nairobi to meet him, and on our drive back was happy to find that he did not seem to have developed any resentment against Elsa, or fear of her, in spite of her peculiar behavior toward him during his last visit.

I had hoped to arrive in camp before she turned up, but in fact we did not get in till suppertime, and found the family in front of the tents, eating. I was a little apprehensive, but Elsa welcomed us both in the most friendly fashion and then returned to her dinner. We spent the rest of the evening within a few yards of her, but she paid no attention to us.

It was very hot indeed, and the bush was depressingly dry, so that even the studio, which is usually cool, was oppressive when we went there next morning and started our work. Although we were much distracted by baboons, antelopes, and various birds, we achieved a lot, and it was not till after tea that we went to look for Elsa. We did not find her on our way out, but as we were returning to camp along a little game path I suddenly felt her and Jespah rubbing themselves against my legs.

Elsa treated Billy just as she did us, but Jespah was greatly intrigued by his white socks and tennis shoes. Crouching low and hiding behind every available tuft, he prepared to ambush him; but we intervened, so eventually he became disgusted at being thwarted and went off and joined the other cubs. Elsa spent the evening on the roof of the Land Rover.

Next morning she woke me up by licking me through my torn mosquito net. How had she gotten into my tent? I was worried in case she might also have tried to visit Billy, and shouted to him. He replied that Elsa had only just left him. At this moment the Toto arrived with my morning tea. Seeing him, Elsa stepped slowly off my bed and moved to the wicker gate of the thorn enclosure. There she waited until the Toto pushed it aside for her; then she walked out sedately, collected the cubs, and they all trotted off toward the Big Rock.

I dressed quickly and went with some apprehension to find out how Billy had fared. When I saw him grinning at me from inside the wired sleeper I felt better. He told me that Elsa had squeezed her way through the wicker gate of his enclosure, which we had barricaded with thorn, and had then jumped onto the Land Rover. Only when she realized that she couldn't get at him had she gone off to visit me.

She had never paid the slightest attention to David Attenborough or to Jeff, who had slept in the same position. The only people whose beds she insisted on sharing were George's and mine, so I interpreted her behavior toward Billy as a great compliment. I don't know whether he felt the same about it.

In the afternoon we visited the family, which we found on the Whuffing Rock. As soon as Elsa and Jespah spotted us, they came down and gave us a great welcome. Gopa and Little Elsa stayed on the rock, but after we had walked some hundred yards into the bush Elsa called them and they came down, but kept out of our sight. Only when we reached the river did they appear, and then they behaved very quietly, sitting in the water to cool themselves while watching us attentively.

Jespah later joined Elsa, and was very affectionate, but on our way home his antics delayed us. Although Billy had discarded his white socks, he still fascinated Jespah, who sat himself squarely in front of his feet, looking up at him with the most cheeky expression and making all progress impossible. Billy tried to make a series of detours to avoid him, but in vain, for the next moment Jespah was at his feet again. Elsa intervened once or twice and rolled her son over, but this only encouraged him to be more mischievous. George had gone ahead, but suddenly felt himself clasped from behind by two paws and nearly tumbled over. Jespah certainly had a good evening's fun! It was only when we reached camp and he settled down to his dinner that we were left in peace.

October 12 was the last day which Billy was to spend in camp, so we made a determined effort to find the family, failed, but on our return we found Elsa and Jespah in camp. Billy patted Elsa as she lay on the Land Rover and stroked her head, something which as a rule she allows only me to do.

Before Billy left Kenya we decided to show him the Tana, the largest river in Kenya. On our way we passed a baobab tree that is the largest in the area and, judging from its size, may be as much as eight hundred years old. It has two big openings high enough above the ground to provide a safe refuge; they lead into a "cave" which could hold eight or ten people. When George first saw this tree it was being used as a poachers' hide-out. He put a stop to that, but there are still a lot of wooden pegs in its walls, which must have served either as ladders or to hang things on. The openings have at some time been artificially enlarged, and the texture of their surface suggests that this was done a long time ago — perhaps two or three hundred years.

Suddenly we heard dogs barking, and I saw George pick up a rifle and rush off in the direction from which the noise came. He plunged through the inflowing stream and disappeared into a doum-palm thicket; simultaneously two waterbuck jumped into the river, followed by yelping dogs, who soon overtook the swimming antelopes and fixed their fangs into the backs and throats of their victims. The smaller buck had three dogs hanging on to it and was struggling desperately. Next we heard a shot, and a dog fell back into the river. Then we saw an African surface. But when he caught sight of Billy and me standing on the bank he dived back into the water.

I was very worried, as the Tana is not only infested by crocodiles, but there are several dangerous whirlpools at this spot. And besides that, there were eight hippos lying straight across the poacher's course. George, too, must have realized this, for he put several bullets on the far side of the swimmer to indicate to him that he had better turn back.

But undeterred by bullets, hippos, crocs, and whirlpools, the poacher swam on, determined to make his escape. The hippos had submerged, and we expected a tragedy to happen every moment; but the man, following the waterbuck and the dogs, made his way to the far bank and landed unharmed. Having done so, he at once disappeared into the bush. Now another poacher appeared, and with him more dogs. They were pursuing a small antelope, who sought the safety of the river in vain, for one dog got hold of its muzzle and tried to suffocate it, while another hung on to its back. George shot both these dogs, and the antelope bravely swam on for a hundred yards, but then sank and drowned.

By now the Tana flowed peacefully, carrying with it the bodies of victims and aggressors alike, sacrificed to man's hunting instinct — or, perhaps, to his greed for meat or money. I was sad that this tragic episode should be Billy's last impression of Kenya.

The cubs cross the river.

Baby Crocs
and Grown Cubs

DURING the second week of October the fierce lioness and her mate announced their arrival by impressive roarings from the Big Rock. Elsa took the hint and at once moved her family across the river.

One evening at about 8:30 P.M., two lions started roaring. All the family listened intently, but only Elsa and Jespah trotted quickly toward the studio. Gopa and Little Elsa, after going a short way with them, came back to finish their meal. They went on gorging until there was a frightening roaring — so close that they rushed at full speed after their mother, who by now had crossed the river. I brought the remains of their meal into safety, which was as well, for the lion duet went on all through the night.

The following afternoon, when the light was already fading, Makedde and I saw a lioness climbing up the Big Rock and then sitting on top of it — undoubtedly this was the fierce lioness. I got my field glasses and had my first good look at her. She was much darker and heavier than Elsa, and rather ugly. I observed that she was staring at us.

Suddenly there was a scream close to us, and the next moment the bush seemed alive with elephants. Makedde and I ran back to the camp as fast as we could. All that evening the elephants trumpeted and rumbled as they went down to the river to drink. Besides this, the lioness kept on roaring from the top of the rock. There was no question of sleep that night, and Elsa naturally kept away.

In the morning we tracked the fierce lioness' pugmarks and those of her mate; they had gone upstream, back to the area in which we believed they usually lived. Elsa no doubt knew this, for that night she brought the family into camp for their dinner. She now paid little attention to me until the cubs had settled down to their meal; then she was as affectionate as ever.

The air was oppressive, and lightning streaked the horizon at frequent intervals. Soon after I had gone to bed, a strong wind started blowing; the trees creaked and the canvas of the tent flapped. Then the first drops of rain fell, and it was not long before I seemed to be under a waterspout. The downpour continued throughout the night. We had not expected this deluge and had not hammered our tent pegs in; as a result the poles collapsed and I spent my time trying to raise them sufficiently to keep some shelter over my head, while a river seemed to run around my feet.

When at last the freezing hours came to an end with daybreak, I looked forward to a cup of hot tea to warm me up; but none appeared, for the firewood was too wet to kindle, and besides, the boys had spent the night in the same condition as myself.

When I emerged I saw that George's tent had also collapsed, and from inside it I heard Elsa moaning in a low voice. Soon she appeared with Jespah and Gopa, rather bedraggled but dry. But even this downpour had not induced Little Elsa to seek shelter, and when I caught sight of her outside the thorn fence I saw that she was drenched.

I began to sort out our soaked belongings and remove them to the cars to save them from the lions, and in this I was "helped" by Jespah, who had great fun defending each box I wanted to move. When I had finished my work, Elsa, Jespah, and Gopa crowded into the tent with me. Little Elsa consented to come inside the flaps but no farther; at least she had some protection there.

The rain continued for four days, with only short respites in the late afternoons; visibility was reduced to a few yards. This was nothing unusual, for the rains vary a great deal in this part of Kenya. A hilly area may have a rainfall of a hundred inches in the year, while the surrounding plains record only fifteen inches.

Elsa's home, though in semidesert country, benefits from a nearby mountain range from which several small streams run into the arid region. The one nearest to the camp now rose higher than I had ever seen it. A roaring red torrent thundered over its banks and flooded the studio up to the level of the table, depositing a great deal of debris including a doum palm which had been uprooted. I was exceedingly glad that Elsa and the cubs were on our side of the river and that we had sufficient food for them.

When the rains stopped after a week, I observed many baby animals. But the queerest nursery of all I discovered one morning when I was walking down the river. Close to one of Elsa's favorite crossing places is a deep pool, where I observed what seemed to be gigantic tadpoles; they kept in a vertical position by paddling energetically. When I looked at them closely I saw that they were baby crocs; they must have measured no more than seven inches and could not have been more than two or three days old. They kept close to the steep bank and sometimes climbed up it. With their muddy coloring and large black blotches they were perfectly camouflaged. We counted nine of them swimming close together within about a square yard. One, however, seemed to act as sentry; it sometimes ventured on short excursions into the river, but always returned very quickly.

We tried to find the broken eggshells from which the crocs had hatched, but failed to do so; perhaps they were born on the other side of the river, which we could not cross on account of the flood. Two days later we returned to the place and saw only a couple of baby crocs, and on our next visit there was only one left.

George reached camp as soon as the condition of the ground made it possible for him to travel, and he brought five Game Scouts with him. They were to provide a permanent patrol and put down poaching. It was necessary that they should live some distance away from Elsa and from our camp, so George now began supervising the establishment of their post and cutting a motor track to it.

In two weeks' time we hoped that this work would be well advanced; then we would start deserting Elsa for increasingly long periods, so as to compel the cubs to go hunting with her and assume their true wild life. Our unexpectedly prolonged stay in the bush had caused them to get a little too used to camp life, though we had no control over them. Jespah was now on quite intimate terms with us; but all the cubs' wild instincts were intact, and certainly Gopa and Little Elsa only put up with us because they saw that their mother insisted that we were friends.

We wondered whether Elsa communicated her wish that they should not hurt us, which they were now well equipped to do, or whether they simply followed her example. Jespah in particular, when he was playing with us, or when he was jealous, could have done a lot of damage if he had not controlled himself; but he always did so, and even when he was in a temper, gave us good warning of the fact.

Gopa was less friendly, but so long as we left him alone he did nothing to provoke an incident. Little Elsa remained shy, though she now seemed less nervous of us than she used to be.

We were surprised that none of the cubs ever attempted to follow Elsa onto the roof of the Land Rover, though they often gazed up at their mother with disappointed expressions when she was resting on the canvas to escape their teasing. Judging by their ability to climb trees, they could very easily have jumped onto the hood and then taken another leap onto the roof — and indeed Elsa had done this at a younger age — but for some reason they seemed to regard the Land Rover as out of bounds.

During George's absence, Jespah and Gopa used his tent as a sort of den. As a result, on his return he found it rather crowded at night. I was a little worried: George prefers to sleep on a low hounds-field bed, and with Elsa, Jespah, and Gopa around it I wondered whether there might not be trouble at night, but they behaved remarkably well. Whenever Jespah tried to play with his toes, George's authoritative "No" made him stop at once.

The extent to which they felt at home was illustrated when one night Elsa rolled around and tipped over George's bed, throwing him on top of Jespah. No commotion followed, and Gopa, who was sleeping near George's head, did not even move.

A day later, when we were returning to camp, we found the family, except for Jespah, gorging on a carcass. It was not long before we discovered the missing cub behind the tents, enjoying a roast guinea fowl which he had stolen off the table. But he had such a mischievous expression that we could do nothing but laugh at the little rascal. We were surprised, however, that he preferred cooked meat to fresh.

Next day we had a further surprise when we came across the family in the bush and found the cubs being suckled. They were now ten and a half months old, and I do not think they could have gotten much milk, as Elsa's teats seemed to be empty.

Although they were still being suckled, we now noticed the first signs of adolescence in Jespah and Gopa. They had grown fine fluff around their faces and necks, and if they looked a bit unshaven, their appearance was certainly very endearing. Elsa greeted us warmly, and Jespah pushed himself between us and demanded to be patted too. Elsa watched us and then licked her son approvingly.

We walked back to camp together. In front of it were the remains of last evening's meal, but Elsa refused even to sniff at it, and demanded a new kill. Later a leopard grunted from the other side of the river, and this caused her to rush off. The cubs followed her after about fifteen minutes. We were very glad to see that Elsa now took the initiative and was prepared to defend her territory.

That night a lion roared; and when we later traced his pugmarks, they led to the Big Rock. Evidently something had given the cubs a fright, for on November 24, when Elsa swam over, they refused to follow her; she had to go back twice to encourage them before they too swam across. Once landed, they had a great game, Elsa rolling Jespah round and round like a bundle, which he loved, and poor Gopa jumping clumsily between them, asking to be noticed. When I came closer to photograph them, Gopa growled at me, whereupon Jespah gave him such a clout that Gopa looked quite stupefied by his punishment. It was all done in fun, but it showed up the different characters of the brothers. But as always, when they settled down to their dinner all jealousy was forgotten.

George had shot a guinea fowl, and I brought it out behind my back because I wanted to give it to Little

Elsa. She took in the situation at once, and while continuing to eat with her brothers, watched me carefully as I walked a little distance away. I waited until Jespah and Gopa were concentrating upon the meat, and when only Little Elsa saw what I was doing, dropped the bird behind a bush. Then, when she alone was watching me, I kept on pointing from her to the guinea fowl, until suddenly she rushed like a streak of lightning, seized the bird, and took it into a thicket where she could eat it unmolested by the others.

Jespah, in his playful moods, liked acting the clown. One day when he was being especially lively, teasing everybody and asking for a game, I placed a round wooden tea tray in a branch that hangs over the river, to see what he would do about it. He climbed up and tried to grip the inch-thick rim between his teeth, using one paw to steady it as it swayed. When he got a sufficiently good grip to carry in horizontally, he came down very cautiously, pausing several times to make sure that we were watching him. Finally he reached the ground and then paraded around with his trophy, until Little Elsa and Gopa chased him and put an end to his performance.

George's leave was coming to an end, and this seemed to be the right time for us to leave the camp. Elsa had by now got the upper hand of the fierce lioness and was able to defend her territory. The poachers seemed to have left the district, and we hoped they would not return. By the next drought, the Game Scouts would be able to deal with them, as their post was nearly completed and their patrols were already in action along the river. Besides, the cubs were now powerful young lions, and it was time that they should hunt with their mother and live their natural life.

We decided to space our absences. On the first occasion we had intended to leave for only six days, but in fact, because of very heavy rains, it was nine before I could return. I came alone and greatly missed George's help when I found myself obliged to dig the truck and the Land Rover out of the bog, a task that occupied us for two days.

Elsa did not turn up in answer to the shots we fired; nor were there any signs of spoor around the camp, but these might well have been washed away by the flooding of the river. After a while, I walked toward the Big Rock and came upon Elsa trotting along with the cubs; they were panting and had probably come a long way in answer to my signal. They were delighted to see me, and Jespah struggled to get between Elsa and myself so as to receive his share of the welcome. Gopa and Little Elsa, however, kept their distance.

All were in excellent condition and as fat as they had been when we left. Elsa had a few bites on her chin and neck, but nothing serious. Gopa had grown a much longer and darker mane then Jespah, whose coloring was very light in comparison to his brother's. In a year's time, I thought, what a handsome pride they would make, with two slender, graceful lionesses, accompanied by one blond and one dark lion.

I had brought a carcass, and Elsa settled down to it. But the cubs were in no hurry to eat, and played about for some time before joining her. When she had had her fill, she came over to me and was very affectionate; as the cubs were then too busy eating to notice their mother, there were no demonstrations of jealousy.

How anxious Elsa was to prevent rows or ill-feeling was clearly shown next day. I had given the cubs a guinea fowl and was watching them fighting over it. Gopa growled most alarmingly at Jespah, Little Elsa, and myself. Hearing this, Elsa instantly rushed up to see what was going on, but as soon as she had satisfied herself that nothing serious had provoked Gopa, she returned to the roof of the Land Rover.

A few minutes later, while the cubs were still eating, I went up to Elsa; she snarled at me and spanked me twice. I retired immediately, surprised, as I did not think I had deserved such treatment. Soon afterward Elsa jumped off the car and rubbed herself affectionately against me, obviously wishing to make up for her bad behavior. I stroked her and she settled down beside me, keeping one paw against me. But when the cubs joined us she rolled onto the other side, and I ceased to exist for her.

She constantly showed how anxious she was for the cubs to be friends with us. One evening, after having gorged himself on the meat we had provided, Jespah came into the tent. He was too full to play, and rolled onto his back because his bulging belly was more comfortable in that position. He looked at me, plainly demanding to be patted. As he was in a docile mood, I felt comparatively safe from his swiping paws and sharp claws, so I stroked his silky fur. He closed his eyes and made a sucking noise, a sure sign of contentment. Elsa, who had been watching us from the roof of the car, joined us and licked both Jespah and me, showing how glad she was to see us on such good terms.

This happy scene was abruptly ended by Gopa; he sneaked up and sat on top of Elsa with a most possessive expression, which left me in no doubt that I was not wanted. So I withdrew a short distance and sketched the lions.

Fond as Elsa was of her children, she never failed to discipline them when they were doing something of which she knew we disapproved, even when they were acting only in accordance with their natural instincts.

We usually kept the goats locked up inside my truck at night, but for a short time we were obliged to secure them inside a strong thorn enclosure because the truck had to go away for repairs. During this time Jespah on one occasion beseiged the *boma* so persistently that we were worried for the safety of the goats. All the tricks we invented to divert his attention failed to produce any effect. Then Elsa came to our aid. She pranced around her son, trying to entice him away, but he paid no attention to her; then she spanked him repeatedly. He spanked back. It was amusing to watch the two outwitting each other. Finally Jespah forgot all about the goats and followed Elsa into the tent, where their dinner was waiting for them.

But when he had finished his meal, Jespah, having been cheated of his fun with the goats, looked for other amusement. He found a can of milk, which he rolled across the groundsheet of the tent until it was covered with a sticky mess. Then he took George's pillow, but the feathers tickled him, so he looked for another toy. Before I could stop him, he seized a needle case which I was using and raced out into the dark with it. I was terrified that it would open under the pressure of his jaws and that he might swallow its contents, so I grabbed our supper, a roast guinea fowl, and ran after him. Luckily, the sight of the bird proved too much for him; he dropped the case, scattering the needles, pins, razor blades, and scissors over the grass. We carefully collected them so they should not prove a danger to the cubs.

Taking the kill across the river.

Play-fighting was the cubs' favorite sport.

The cubs pose together.

A New Year Begins

IT was now time for us to go back to Isiolo and leave the cubs to a spell of wild life.

On December 3 I called on the District Commissioner in whose area Elsa's home lies. I wanted to give him the latest news of the cubs and to ask his advice as to how I could best use some of the royalties of *Born Free* to help develop the game reserve in which she was living.

Elsa was an asset to the reserve because her story had aroused world-wide sympathy and understanding for wild life, and also because part of the money I had received for her book had contributed to the sum needed to establish the new game post. On the other hand, the tribesmen blamed her for the stricter supervision of poaching due to our presence. Furthermore, a woman had recently been killed in Tanganyika by a tame lion, and the District Commissioner now told me that the incident had been used to stimulate ill-feeling against Elsa. Also it was claimed that her friendship for us, by accustoming her to humans, could make her a danger to strangers. He warned me that, under the circumstances, it might become necessary to remove Elsa from her home.

Four days later a rumor reached us that two tribesmen had been mauled by a lion fourteen miles from Elsa's camp. George left at once to investigate. He reached camp too late to pursue his inquiries, but when daylight came he went to the Game Scout post. No one there had heard of any tribesmen being mauled by a lion, so he sent the Scouts to the scene of the alleged accident and returned to camp.

In order to keep Elsa and the cubs near the tents, he gave them a carcass, which they dragged into a bush close by. They stayed there until the evening.

The day after George's hurried departure for the camp, I followed, bringing the truck as well as the Land Rover. It was late when we arrived, and the men were too tired to unload the truck and put the goats into it for the night. We therefore secured them in a thorn enclosure.

Although our arrival was noisy and Elsa must have heard us, she did not come to welcome me. This was the first time she had failed to do so.

After I had gone to bed, I heard the cubs attacking the goats' *boma*. Sounds of breaking wood, growling lions, and stampeding animals bleating left no doubt as to what was happening. We rushed out, but not before Elsa, Gopa, and Little Elsa had each killed a goat. Jespah was holding one down with his paw, which George was able to rescue unhurt. It took us two hours to round up the bolting, panic-stricken survivors of the herd and secure them in the truck, while hyenas, attracted by the noise, circled around.

Elsa took her kill across the river. George, who followed, saw a large crocodile going after Elsa, and shot at it but missed. He remained sitting close to Elsa until 2 A.M. to see if the croc would reappear, but it did not. The cubs were very much upset at finding themselves and their kills separated from Elsa by the river; after half an hour of anxious miaowing they joined their mother without having started to eat the goats they had killed.

In the afternoon the Game Scouts returned; they had no confirmation of the rumor that tribesmen had been mauled by lions, but they had collected plenty of evidence to show that, influenced by poachers and political agitators, the tribesmen were becoming increasingly hostile toward Elsa. We realized that her life was in danger, and discussed what we should do.

We had spent six months in camp — much longer than we had originally planned — in order to protect Elsa and her cubs from poachers, and by doing so had inevitably interfered with the lions' natural life. If now we stayed on, the cubs would become so tame that they would have little chance of adapting themselves in the future to the life of the bush.

Besides this, if we went on camping in the reserve we should only increase the antagonism of the tribesmen. Since we could not, in the circumstances, leave Elsa and the cubs alone, the only solution we could think of was to look for a new home for them and move them as soon as possible.

We had had great difficulty in finding a suitable place

for Elsa's release; to find one for her and the cubs was likely to be still more difficult. We knew that by now, with their mother's help in teaching them to hunt and in protecting them from natural foes, they were capable of living the life of the bush. But where would they be safe, not only from wild animals but also from man, who now proved to be their most dangerous enemy? Leaving me in charge of the camp, George returned the next morning to Isiolo, hoping to find a solution to this problem.

In the afternoon I walked with Nuru to the Whuffing Rock, where we had spotted Elsa. She came down at once to greet us; but when I started to climb up the saddle to join the sleeping cubs, she prevented me from doing so by sitting squarely across my path, and only after we were on our way home did she call her children. Through my field glasses I saw Jespah and Gopa climbing down, but Little Elsa remained on top like a sentry.

When it was dark, the family arrived in camp; and after eating their dinner, Elsa and her sons played happily in the tent until they dozed off in a close embrace. I sketched them, while Little Elsa watched us from outside the tent. In the night a lion called, and for the next three days he kept close to the camp. During this time Elsa stayed in the immediate vicinity.

I usually met the family on their way to camp, and was often touched by Jespah's behavior. When Elsa and I greeted each other he didn't want to be left out, but I think he knew that I was scared of his claws, for he would place himself with his rear toward me and keep absolutely still, as though to assure me that in this way I would be quite safe from accidental scratches while I patted him.

From then on he always adopted this attitude when he wanted to be stroked.

By now the rains should have ended, but we still had some wet days. Thanks to this the bush had remained greener than it usually is in December.

After dark, one rainy day, when the river was still in flood, I heard two lions roaring upstream. Elsa replied to them. Much later I heard the cubs in front of my tent. The lions went on roaring throughout most of the night. Elsa and the cubs crossed the flooded river in the early morning; it was plain that they wished to avoid the two lions.

December 20 was the cubs' first birthday. It began anxiously, for the river was too high to cross, so we could not discover whether Elsa was all right after the excitements of the night. I was very happy when, about teatime, the family turned up. They were wet but unharmed.

As a birthday treat I had a guinea fowl, which I cut up into four portions so that each should have a share. After gobbling these tidbits, Elsa hopped onto the Land Rover while the cubs tore at some meat we had prepared for them.

As all the lions were happily occupied, I called to Makedde to escort me for a walk. As soon as we set out, Elsa jumped off the car and followed us. Then Jespah, seeing his mother disappear, stopped his meal and ran after us. And we had not gone far before I saw Gopa and Little Elsa, parallel to us, chasing each other through the bush. When we came to the place where the track comes nearest to the Big Rock, the lions sat down and rolled in the sand. I waited for a little while and watched the setting sun turn the rock to a bright red; then, since Elsa looked settled, I walked back, expecting the family to spend the evening on the rock. I was surprised when she followed me. She kept close, so that I could help with the tsetse flies, and Jespah trotted next to us like a well-trained child. Gopa and Little Elsa took their time; they scampered about a long way behind us, and we often had to stop to wait for them.

Elsa seemed to have come along just to join me in my walk; this was the first time she had done so since the cubs were born. I thought it a charming way of celebrating their birthday.

When we arrived in camp, Elsa flung herself on the ground inside my tent and was joined by her sons, who nuzzled and embraced their mother with their paws. I sketched them until Elsa retired to the roof of the Land Rover and the cubs started to eat their dinner. When I was sure that the cubs would not observe me, I went over to Elsa and stroked her, and she responded very affectionately. I wanted to thank her for having shared her children with us during their first year, and for having shared her anxieties during the period which is so full of dangers for any young animals. But as though to remind me that in spite of our friendship we belonged to two different worlds, after I had been with her for some time a lion suddenly started roaring, and after listening intently Elsa left.

Elsa and the cubs spent the night of December 23 in camp, and after breakfast, when I strolled along the road to read in the sand the report on last night's visitors, she and the cubs followed me. I called to Makedde, and we

Elsa and her cubs came for a walk with us.

all walked along together for about two miles.

Jespah was particularly friendly, brushing against me, and even standing quite still while I removed a tick which was close to one of his eyes.

We went on till we came to a rain pool, where the lions had a drink. By now the sun was getting hot, and it would not have surprised me if Elsa had decided to spend the day in this place, but good-naturedly she turned back when we did and trotted slowly home with us.

I could not help feeling as though we were all taking our Sunday family walk. Though in fact this was the morning of Christmas Eve, and Elsa could have no knowledge of special days, by a strange coincidence she had chosen a day I felt the need to commemorate, by coming for a walk with me and bringing her family with her.

Elsa and the cubs were feeling the increasing heat very much, and often stopped under the shade of a tree to rest. Yet when we came near the Big Rock they suddenly rushed at full speed through the bush, and in a few leaps reached the top; there they settled among the boulders. I scrambled after them as best I could, but Elsa made it quite plain that I should now leave them alone. She always knew exactly how much she felt it was fitting for her to give to each of her two worlds, so I confined myself to taking some photographs of her guarding her cubs.

George arrived about teatime with a suitcase full of mail. While we strolled about picking flowers for Christmas decorations, he told me of the inquiries he had made about finding a new home for Elsa and the cubs. He thought that the Lake Rudolf area would be the place in which the lions would be safest from human interference. He had obtained permission from the authorities to take them there if the need arose, and was soon going to reconnoiter the region to find a suitable spot.

This part of Kenya is very grim, and conditions are tough there, so I felt depressed at the prospect. Elsa chose this moment to join us on our way home; behind her the cubs were playing happily along the road. I could not bear to visualize them roaming on the windswept, lava-strewn desert which surrounds the lake.

When we reached camp we gave the family their supper, which kept them occupied while I arranged the table for our Christmas dinner. I decorated it with flowers and tinsel ornaments and put the little silver Christmas tree I had kept from last year in the middle. Then I brought out the presents for George and the boys.

Jespah watched my preparations very carefully. The moment I turned my back to get the candles he rushed up and seized a parcel which contained a shirt for George, and bounced off with it into a thicket. Gopa joined him immediately, and the two of them had a wonderful time with the shirt. When at last we rescued it, it was in no state to be given to George.

By now it was nearly dark, and I started to light the candles. That was all Jespah needed to make him decide to come and help me. I only just managed to prevent him from pulling the tablecloth, with the decorations and burning candles, on top of himself. It needed a lot of coaxing to make him keep away so that I could light the rest of the candles. When all was ready he came up, tilted his head, looked at the glittering Christmas tree, and then sat down and watched the candles burn lower and lower.

As each flame went out I felt as though another happy day of our life in the camp had passed. A few yards away, Elsa and her cubs rested peacefully in the grass, hardly visible in the fading light.

Afterward George and I read our mail. It took us many hours to do so, and brought us close to all the people who were wishing Elsa and her family and us happiness.

Mercifully, it was one of the last envelopes I opened which contained an order for the removal of Elsa and her cubs from the reserve.

ELSA'S CAMP, DECEMBER 24, 1960

Postscript

A month after Joy Adamson finished this book, Elsa died in the bush after an illness lasting several days. A post-mortem established that her death was caused by babesia, a parasite that destroys the red corpuscles.

The cubs immediately became very wild and, for a few weeks, only came to the camp after dark to be fed. Then they disappeared.

Shortly afterward the Adamsons learned that they had been attacking goats belonging to local tribesmen, and it became essential to catch them and move them to an uninhabited area. This highly difficult operation, which involved trapping the cubs and transporting them seven hundred miles to the Serengeti National Game Park, in Tanganyika, was achieved in May, 1961.

DATE DUE

MAY 2 0 2009		
JUN 0 4 2009		
JUN 2 2 2009		
JUL 2 8 2009		
AUG 1 9 2009		
SEP 0 3 2009		
OCT 2 2 2009		
NOV 0 3 2009		
DEC 1 4 2009		
APR 0 2 2010		
MAY 1 6 2012		
NOV 0 6 2017		